COOKING WITH
Bon Appétit

COOKING WITH
Bon Appétit

Beef, Veal, Lamb & Pork

THE KNAPP PRESS
Publishers
Los Angeles

Copyright © 1984 by Knapp Communications Corporation

Published by The Knapp Press
5900 Wilshire Boulevard, Los Angeles, California 90036

Library of Congress Cataloging in Publication Data

Main entry under title:

Beef, veal, lamb & pork.

  (Cooking with Bon appétit)
  Includes index.
  1. Cookery (Meat) I. Bon appétit. II. Title: Beef, veal, lamb and pork. III. Series.
TX749.B385 1984   641.6'6   84-19405
ISBN 0-89535-138-2

On the cover: *Steak with Red Peppers and Sun-dried Tomatoes*

Printed and bound in the United States of America

10   9   8   7   6   5

🍃 Contents

❧ Foreword

When a royal feast is called for, nothing surpasses a majestic prime rib of beef or a regal crown roast of lamb. In the summer, steaks, ribs, or burgers tossed on the grill are the height of casual entertaining. And in winter, there's no dish more wholesome or heartwarming than a robust beef stew or a delicate braise of veal.

Whatever or whenever the occasion, beef, veal, lamb and pork are still undisputed main course favorites. And no wonder. As a group, these red meats encompass a great diversity of dishes. That diversity is celebrated here, with more than 200 outstanding recipes from the pages of *Bon Appétit* magazine—recipes excitingly innovative and comfortably familiar, down-home favorites and authentic creations from exotic cuisines, quick or make-ahead dishes and spectacular showpieces worth a little extra effort for truly special meals.

To help you locate just the right dish for any occasion, the beef, veal, lamb, and pork recipes here are organized into chapters by kind of meat and, within each chapter, by cooking method. There are grilled and broiled dishes, from Steaks with Zesty Tarragon Butter (page 2) to the spicy Indonesian Skewered Barbecued Lamb (page 61). In the sections on frying and sautéing you'll find such specialties as Hamburgers with Garlic-Basil Butter (page 8), Veal Chops with Mushroom Sauce (page 33) and Miniature Lamb Patties with Sauce Basquaise (page 68). Roasted and baked dishes include Butterflied Leg of Lamb with Parmesan Crust (page 73), and Roasted Spareribs with Hoisin-Honey Glaze (page 92). Among the poached, braised and stewed dishes are recipes as widely varied as British Steak and Kidney Pie (page 19), a Moroccan Lamb Tajine with Dates (page 83), Boiled Beef in Ale (page 27), and Braised Pork with Pears (page 107).

Throughout this volume, you'll find a wealth of special features to help build your kitchen expertise. You'll learn how to prepare a Classic Brown Sauce and its variations (page 38) and a Béarnaise to grace grilled steaks (page 66). There are also expert tips on preparing perfect Brown Stock (page 44), and a complete glossary of meat cooking methods (page 5). It's a feast of information to accompany a true feast of memorable recipes from *Bon Appétit.*

1 ❦ Beef

Beef means hearty eating. Its rich, robust flavor, deep red color, and firm texture satisfy like no other food, and cuisines the world over recognize it as a symbol of abundant generosity. From the traditional English Roast Beef with Yorkshire Pudding (page 16) to spicy Texas-style ribs with barbecue sauce (page 3), the satisfying French country Pot-au-feu (page 27) to the broiled kebabs marinated in onion, lemon and cumin (page 4), beef makes dining a most special occasion.

These and other beef classics can be found in this chapter, along with a delightful variety of exciting new recipes that show off beef's remarkable versatility. Want a change from the usual grilled steak? Try serving it with a sauce of red peppers, ricotta cheese and sun-dried tomatoes (page 6), or marinated with garlic, ginger and soy sauce and barbecued (page 2). Something elegant yet easy to prepare? Filet Mignon with Mushrooms and Prosciutto (page 12) or Mexican Beef Fillet with Tomato-Orange Cumin Sauce (page 26) are both ready to serve in little more than half an hour. Want something different for a casual family meal? Look no further than Hamburgers with Garlic-Basil Butter (page 8), Brisket with Prunes (page 17) or an Italian-style Meat Loaf with Three Cheeses (page 18).

When selecting beef, as with any meat, you should consider several factors. If the meat has been "aged" for several weeks under controlled temperature and humidity, it will have better flavor and be more tender than unaged beef, but will pay a higher price for its storage time and loss of weight during aging. Best for grilling, frying and roasting are the more tender cuts from the animal's ribs, loin and rump; the finest cuts will be richly marbled with streaks of firm white fat, which baste the meat from within during cooking. But you may prefer less marbled meat which, though somewhat tougher, will also be lower in calories. For braising or stewing, the best cuts of beef are the tougher cuts from the neck, shoulder, legs, brisket and flank. Coming from more developed muscles with a lower concentration of fat, they require long, moist cooking to make them tender, and their richer flavor mingles wonderfully with the cooking liquid.

❦ Grilling and Broiling

Steaks with Zesty Tarragon Butter

6 servings

2 medium shallots
2 tablespoons chopped fresh parsley
4 teaspoons tarragon vinegar
½ teaspoon dried tarragon

½ teaspoon freshly ground pepper
½ cup (1 stick) butter, cut into small pieces, well chilled

6 beef tenderloin steaks

Combine shallots, parsley, vinegar, tarragon and pepper in processor and mince using several on/off turns. Add butter and blend well. Transfer to waxed paper and form into cylinder. Refrigerate or freeze until firm.

Grill, broil or panfry steaks to desired doneness. Transfer to individual plates. Slice butter evenly into 6 rounds (or thinner if desired). Set atop steaks and serve immediately.

Teriyaki Steak

4 servings

4 small ¾-inch-thick New York strip steaks *or* one 2- to 3-pound flank steak, trimmed and scored
1¼ cups firmly packed light brown sugar
1 cup soy sauce

1 ½-inch piece fresh ginger, peeled and grated
½ garlic clove, crushed
⅛ teaspoon sesame oil

Arrange steaks in shallow dish. Combine brown sugar, soy sauce, ginger, garlic and sesame oil and blend well. Pour over steaks. Cover and marinate in refrigerator at least 3 hours or overnight, turning occasionally. Broil or barbecue to desired doneness. (If using flank steak, slice diagonally across grain before serving.)

Barbecued Marinated Steak

8 to 12 servings

¾ cup dry red wine
1 large onion, minced
½ cup chopped fresh parsley
2 large garlic cloves, minced
1 bay leaf
1 teaspoon dried tarragon

1 teaspoon dried thyme
½ teaspoon freshly ground pepper
Dash of hot pepper sauce
2 beef sirloin steaks, 4 to 5 pounds each, cut 2 inches thick

Combine ingredients for marinade in heavyweight, large plastic bag. Add meat. Seal bag securely and rotate several times. Let marinate at cool room temperature 4 hours, turning often. Prepare barbecue. Cook meat (preferably to rare or medium-rare stage), basting often with marinade. Carve steak diagonally into thin slices to serve.

Texas-style Hickory-smoked Beef Ribs with Panhandle Barbecue Sauce

Cooking ribs with smoke is very much a Western tradition. This tangy basting sauce adds just the right touch of spice. If hickory chips are not available, use chips from any other hardwood.

6 to 8 servings

Panhandle Barbecue Sauce
1 cup bottled chili sauce
3 tablespoons minced onion
2 tablespoons minced green bell pepper
1 tablespoon firmly packed brown sugar
1 fresh *or* canned jalapeño chili, minced

1 teaspoon dry mustard
2 dashes Worcestershire sauce

5 pounds beef ribs, cut from rib of beef and trimmed (do not use short ribs)

For barbecue sauce: Combine chili sauce, onion, green pepper, brown sugar, jalapeño, mustard and Worcestershire sauce in small pan and bring to boil. Reduce heat and simmer 15 minutes.

Soak 3 cups of hickory chips 15 minutes in enough water to cover. Remove and drain well.

Heat coals until gray ash forms. Spread into single layer and let burn about 30 minutes. Set grill 4 inches above coals. Arrange ribs on grill. Add about half of hickory chips to fire. Cover barbecue if possible, leaving vents open. Cook ribs about 40 minutes, turning every 10 minutes and adding chips and more coals as needed. After 40 minutes, brush ribs generously with sauce and continue cooking, turning and brushing frequently, for about 20 minutes.

Skewered Beef (Bo Sa Lui)

8 servings

4 heaping teaspoons sugar
3 garlic cloves
2 shallots
4 teaspoons fish sauce (nuoc mam)*
4 teaspoons vegetable oil
3 stalks fresh lemongrass (lower bulb portion only), chopped, *or* 3 tablespoons finely chopped dried (soak in hot water 2 hours, then drain and chop)*
Freshly ground pepper
1½ pounds beef top round *or* sirloin (in 1 piece about 4 inches in diameter), cut into very thin 2 × 2-inch slices

½ package mung bean threads (cellophane noodles)* *or* rice sticks (mai fun)*
2 quarts boiling water
Boston *or* Bibb lettuce leaves
Marinated Carrots (see following recipes)
Nuoc Cham (see following recipes)

Combine sugar, garlic and shallots in mortar and pound into paste or mash with back of spoon in mixing bowl. Add fish sauce, oil, lemongrass and pepper and blend well. Spread on both sides of meat using fingertips. Let stand at room temperature 30 minutes.

Prepare charcoal grill or preheat broiler. Remove any bits of lemongrass clinging to meat. Fold each piece of meat in half and thread about 8 to 10 slices on each skewer. Barbecue or broil until done, turning once, about 3 minutes. Transfer to heated platter and keep warm.

Boil mung bean threads in water 5 minutes. Drain well; rinse under cold water and drain again. Mound on platter next to meat. Arrange lettuce leaves on platter and top with Marinated Carrots. Serve with Nuoc Cham for dipping.

*Available in oriental markets.

Marinated Carrots (Carot Chua)

8 servings

2 medium carrots	2 teaspoons sugar
1 cup water	Dash of salt
2 teaspoons vinegar	

Cut several wedges lengthwise in each carrot and remove. Slice carrots paper thin (slices should resemble flower petals). Combine all remaining ingredients in small bowl and blend well. Add carrots and mix thoroughly. Let stand 1 hour. Drain well before serving.

Nuoc Cham

No Vietnamese meal is served without this tangy sauce, used to add spice to practically everything. It can be refrigerated about 1 week.

Makes about ¾ cup

1 tablespoon plus 2 teaspoons sugar	Juice and pulp of ¼ lime
4 garlic cloves	5 tablespoons water
2 to 4 dried hot chilies *or* 2 fresh chilies	¼ cup fish sauce (nuoc mam)*

Combine sugar, garlic and chilies in mortar and pound into paste or mash with back of spoon in mixing bowl. Add lime juice and pulp and continue blending until well mixed. Add water and fish sauce and mix thoroughly.

*Available in oriental markets.

Beef Shish Kebab in Onion Marinade

4 servings

½ large onion, grated	Salt and freshly ground pepper
¼ teaspoon ground cumin	
¼ teaspoon fresh lemon juice	8 cherry tomatoes (optional)
¼ teaspoon cider vinegar	1 green bell pepper, cored, seeded and cubed
⅛ teaspoon garlic powder	
Dried red pepper flakes (optional)	1 large onion, cubed
1 pound beef top sirloin, cut into 12 cubes	

Combine grated onion, cumin, lemon juice, vinegar, garlic powder and red pepper flakes in small bowl. Season beef generously with salt and pepper. Rub cumin mixture into beef. Set aside 30 minutes.

Preheat broiler or prepare barbecue grill. Alternate meat, tomatoes, green pepper and cubed onion on 4 skewers. Broil or barbecue to desired doneness.

❧ Cooking Terms

Grill or Broil
To place meat on a preheated grill or broiler that sears and cooks the meat while browning it. Thick cuts of meat should be cooked further from the heat at slightly lower temperatures than thinner cuts because they require a longer cooking period. Barbecuing gives an added smoky taste depending on the charcoal or wood used.

Sauté
To cook in just enough fat to keep the food from sticking. Tender and quick-cooking cuts of meat should be used rather than cuts that require long, slow cooking.

- Don't cover the pan when sautéing, since that would steam, rather than sear and create a crisp coating.
- Make sure your sauté pan or skillet is large enough and that the meat is not crowded. Allow enough space to brown the sides of the meat.
- Sauté over medium-high or high heat for best results.

Stir-fry
This method is done in a wok with a small amount of very hot oil. The meat is cut into small pieces, stirred and cooked quickly.

Deep-fry
To fry in deep fat or oil. Remember that vegetable oils burn at about 500°F, while butter burns at about 250°F, so be sure to use a vegetable oil.

Braise
To cook meat in a small amount of liquid that usually has been prebrowned. A mixture of diced vegetables is sautéed and then the meat is returned to the pan or casserole and just enough liquid is added to simmer the meat slowly until tender. The liquid used may be stock, wine or water. This liquid then becomes the base of the sauce.

Poach
To cook meat in a liquid just below the boiling point or at a simmer. The meat will toughen when cooked at a boil. The cooking liquid can be stock, wine, water or any combination.

Roast or Bake
To cook by dry heat. It is important to have the oven temperature high enough to keep any moisture evaporated so that the meat does not steam. The temperature should not be too high, or the meat may dry out. The roasting rack is an excellent aid for this purpose. An instant meat thermometer is extremely helpful to determine the desired degree of doneness.

Marinate
To cook meat in an acid, such as lime juice, lemon juice or wine.

California Marinated Chuck Steak

The secret of this excellent steak is to start with the tenderest cut of the chuck—the first cut right next to the rib portion of the steer. If the meat is aged prime or heavy choice, all the better.

4 to 6 servings

1 cup beer
¼ cup soy sauce
¼ cup pineapple juice
½ small onion, cut into chunks
2 garlic cloves
2 tablespoons firmly packed brown sugar
2 tablespoons vinegar

¼ teaspoon grated fresh ginger
1 3- to 3¼-pound first cut (also known as blade) beef chuck steak, about 2½ to 3 inches thick, trimmed of all fat

Fresh watercress *or* parsley sprigs (garnish)

Puree all ingredients except meat and garnish. Pour marinade over steak. Cover tightly and marinate 24 hours in refrigerator, turning once.

Preheat broiler. Cover bottom of broiler pan with water and set rack in place. Drain marinade from steak. Broil meat about 2 to 4 inches from heat source until browned on each side. Reduce temperature to 375°F and continue cooking about 6 to 8 minutes per side for rare, 8 to 10 minutes for medium rare, and 10 to 12 minutes for medium. Place on heated platter and garnish. Separate meat from bones with sharp knife, then slice.

Steak with Red Peppers and Sun-dried Tomatoes

This delicious entrée is similar to the one served at the Cordon Bleu in Bologna's Grand Hotel Elite.

4 servings

1 large red bell pepper
⅔ cup whole milk ricotta cheese
⅓ cup whipping cream
1 small garlic clove
½ cup diced sun-dried tomatoes (pomodori)

4 1-inch-thick beef steak fillets, patted dry
1½ tablespoons minced fresh basil
4 whole sun-dried tomatoes (pomodori)
Basil leaves

Roast red bell pepper 6 inches from heat source until skin blisters and blackens, turning frequently. Steam in plastic bag 10 minutes. Peel off skin; discard stem and seeds. Rinse red pepper and pat dry; dice and set aside.

Puree ricotta, cream and garlic in processor until very smooth.

Cook diced sun-dried tomatoes and red bell pepper in heavy small saucepan over low heat 3 minutes, stirring occasionally. Gradually blend in ricotta mixture. Cook 5 minutes, stirring occasionally.

Meanwhile, grill, barbecue or sauté steaks to desired doneness. Stir minced basil into ricotta sauce. Transfer steaks to heated plates. Spoon some of sauce alongside each. Top each with whole sun-dried tomato. Garnish with basil leaves and serve.

🍃 Sautéing, Deep-frying and Stir-frying

Flour Tortillas with Beef Filling

8 to 10 servings

1½ tablespoons butter
1½ tablespoons vegetable oil
1 pound beef rib-eye steak, cut into ¼ × ¼ × 3-inch strips, patted dry
1 large onion, halved from root end to stem end, then cut crosswise into thin strips

8 to 10 flour tortillas
Green Chile Salsa (see following recipe)
2 ripe tomatoes, peeled and diced

Heat butter and oil in large skillet over medium-high heat. Add meat and sauté until browned on all sides. Remove from skillet using slotted spoon. Add onion to skillet and sauté until browned and softened. Return meat to skillet and stir just to heat through. Transfer filling to heated platter and serve with tortillas, salsa and tomatoes.

Green Chile Salsa

Tomatillos are a pale green fruit with a distinctive lemon flavor. They also tone down hot chilies.

Salsa can be prepared 1 day ahead and refrigerated.

Makes about 2 to 2½ cups

5 green Anaheim *or* poblano chilies
2 unpeeled garlic cloves

6 tomatillos, husks discarded and fruit quartered
½ avocado, peeled

1 cup Mexican cream*
¼ cup loosely packed cilantro (coriander) leaves
½ to 1 teaspoon salt, or to taste

Roast chilies and garlic cloves 6 inches from heat source until skin blisters and blackens, turning frequently. Steam in plastic bag 10 minutes. Peel skins; discard chili stems and seeds.

Place tomatillos in medium skillet and cook over low heat until softened, 3 to 4 minutes. Transfer to processor. Add chilies, garlic and avocado and mix until smooth. Add cream, cilantro and salt and puree until smooth. Salsa may be served warm or cold.

*For Mexican cream, combine 1 cup sour cream, ½ cup whipping cream and 1 teaspoon fresh lime juice in medium bowl and mix well. Set aside at room temperature to thicken. Refrigerate. Makes about 1½ cups.

Coriander Beef Patties (Saté Daging Giling)

6 servings

1 pound ground beef
1 egg, beaten to blend
1 garlic clove, minced
1 teaspoon ground coriander
½ teaspoon salt, or to taste
¼ teaspoon ground cumin

¼ teaspoon freshly ground pepper
⅛ teaspoon freshly grated nutmeg
3 tablespoons corn oil
Fresh cilantro (coriander) sprigs (garnish)

Lightly mix all ingredients except oil and garnish in large bowl. Shape into six ½-inch-thick patties. *(Can be prepared 1 day ahead.)* Heat oil in heavy large skillet over medium heat. Sauté patties to desired degree of doneness, about 2 minutes on each side for medium. Drain on paper towels, garnish with coriander sprigs and serve immediately.

Hamburgers with Garlic-Basil Butter

2 servings

Garlic-Basil Butter
2 tablespoons (¼ stick) butter, room temperature
1 small garlic clove, minced
1 tablespoon minced fresh basil *or* 1 teaspoon dried
¼ teaspoon fresh lemon juice

Burgers
1 pound ground beef (about 20 percent fat)
Salt and freshly ground pepper
Ice chips
2 tablespoons vegetable oil

For garlic-basil butter: Blend all ingredients in small bowl. Form into 2 small rounds. Refrigerate until ready to use.

For burgers: Divide meat in half. Season with salt and pepper. Form into patties with 1 or 2 ice chips in center, handling gently and as little as possible. Heat oil in heavy medium skillet over medium heat until drop of water sizzles when sprinkled in pan. Add patties, increase heat to high and cook until crisp and brown, about 4 minutes per side. Reduce heat to medium and cook 2 minutes more for rare. (Medium or well-done burgers will take proportionally longer.) Top each with butter round and serve.

Easy Frikadeller

6 to 8 servings

1½ pounds ground beef
½ pound ground pork
2 eggs, beaten
2 medium onions, finely chopped
1⅓ cups whipping cream
¾ cup all purpose flour
1½ teaspoons salt
1 teaspoon freshly ground pepper
2 tablespoons (¼ stick) butter, or more

Combine first 8 ingredients in large bowl and mix thoroughly. Melt butter in large skillet over medium-high heat. Lightly oil tablespoon measure. Drop meat mixture by heaping spoonfuls into skillet (in batches if necessary; *do not crowd*) and brown on both sides, turning often and adding more butter if necessary, about 15 to 20 minutes. Transfer to heated platter and serve.

Steak Tips with Mushrooms and Onions

Any unused garlic butter may be frozen for future use.

3 to 4 servings

Garlic Butter
- 2 cups (4 sticks) butter, room temperature
- ½ head garlic, peeled and minced
- ¼ cup dry white wine
- 1 tablespoon chopped fresh parsley
- ¼ teaspoon freshly ground pepper

- 1 large onion, sliced
- ½ pound mushrooms, sliced

- 1 pound beef tenderloin tips
  Salt and freshly ground pepper
  Garlic powder
  Dash of Sherry

For garlic butter: Combine butter, garlic, wine, parsley and pepper in bowl and mix on low speed of electric mixer until thoroughly blended.

Melt 2 tablespoons garlic butter in large skillet over medium-high heat. Add onion and sauté until golden. Add mushrooms and cook lightly. Transfer to plate and keep warm. Drain and wipe pan.

Season meat with salt and pepper and garlic powder. Melt 1 tablespoon garlic butter in same skillet over medium-high heat. Add meat and sauté to desired doneness. Return onion and mushrooms to pan and stir to blend. Add Sherry and serve immediately. Top with additional garlic butter.

Steak with Bleu Cheese and Mustard Sauce

4 servings

Sauce
- ¾ cup Madeira
- 2 tablespoons minced shallot
- 1 cup whipping cream
- ½ cup beef stock
- ½ cup (1 stick) unsalted butter, room temperature
- 6 ounces bleu cheese, crumbled
- 2 tablespoons Dijon mustard
  Salt
  Dried red pepper flakes

- 4 ¾- to 1-inch-thick Spencer *or* rib eye steaks, room temperature
- 2 tablespoons (¼ stick) unsalted butter
- 2 tablespoons olive oil
- 2 medium onions, thinly sliced
  Salt and freshly ground pepper
- ¼ cup minced fresh parsley
  Paprika

For sauce: Mix Madeira and shallot in heavy small saucepan. Boil over high heat until liquid is reduced to 2 tablespoons. Add cream and stock and boil until reduced to 1 cup. Blend ½ cup butter, bleu cheese and mustard in processor or with back of wooden spoon in small bowl. Whisk into Madeira mixture 2 tablespoons at a time. Simmer until creamy, about 3 minutes. Strain sauce. Season with salt and dried red pepper. *(Can be prepared 1 day ahead to this point and refrigerated. Rewarm over low heat before serving.)*

Pat steaks dry; score fat. Melt 2 tablespoons butter with oil in heavy large skillet over high heat. Add steaks and brown on one side, 3 to 4 minutes. Turn steaks over. Add onions to skillet and stir to coat. Season to taste with salt and pepper. Continue cooking steaks to desired doneness, 3 to 4 minutes longer for medium rare. Transfer steaks and onions to platter. Top with parsley. Sprinkle sauce with paprika and serve separately.

Beef with Pancetta and Gorgonzola

This sauce is also superb with liver.

6 servings

2 tablespoons (¼ stick) butter
2 tablespoons olive oil
2 red onions, sliced into ¼-inch rings
Salt and freshly ground pepper

1 cup whipping cream
2 tablespoons cornstarch
4 ounces Gorgonzola cheese
6 slices pancetta (Italian dry-cured unsmoked bacon), about ⅛-inch thick

2 tablespoons (¼ stick) butter
6 1-inch-thick beef tenderloin, rib *or* sirloin steaks (about 1½ pounds total), patted dry

2 tablespoons minced fresh parsley

Melt 2 tablespoons butter with oil in heavy medium skillet over medium-low heat. Stir in sliced onions. Season with salt and pepper. Cover and cook, stirring frequently, until onions are tender, 10 to 12 minutes. Keep warm.

Gradually blend cream into cornstarch in heavy small saucepan. Bring to boil over low heat, stirring constantly. Remove from heat. Add cheese and stir until smooth. Add salt and pepper to taste. Set sauce aside at room temperature until ready to use.

Cook pancetta slices in heavy large skillet over medium heat until edges begin to curl; *do not cook until crisp.* Remove with slotted spoon. Melt 2 tablespoons butter in same skillet over medium-high heat. Add steaks, searing and browning on one side. Turn and sprinkle with salt and pepper. Continue cooking to desired doneness, 3 to 5 minutes for medium rare. Just before steaks are done, spoon 2 tablespoons sauce over each, then cover skillet so cheese melts quickly. Remove from heat.

To serve, set steaks on pancetta slices. Surround with onions. Sprinkle with minced parsley. Reheat remaining sauce over very low heat or in top of double boiler over gently simmering water. Serve sauce separately.

Norwegian Meat Cakes

Makes about 20 cakes

1 pound lean ground round steak
1 pound lean ground pork
¾ cup fine fresh breadcrumbs
¾ cup hot milk
1 teaspoon ground cardamom
½ teaspoon dried sage

½ teaspoon allspice
½ teaspoon salt
¼ teaspoon freshly ground pepper
¼ teaspoon ground cloves
2 tablespoons (¼ stick) butter

Mix steak, pork and breadcrumbs in large bowl. Add milk 2 tablespoons at a time, blending well after each addition. Combine seasonings in small bowl and add to meat mixture, blending well. Form mixture into 2½-inch patties. Melt butter in large skillet over medium heat. Add patties (in batches if necessary; *do not crowd*) and cook until browned and centers are no longer pink, about 5 minutes on each side. Drain on paper towels and serve.

Steak au Poivre

4 servings

2 18-ounce boneless prime strip
  sirloin steaks cut 2 inches thick
¼ cup coarsely cracked pepper
¾ cup dry red wine

½ cup Cognac
½ cup Glace de Viande (meat glaze)
  (see following recipe)

Trim excess fat from steaks and render in heavy skillet over high heat. Press pepper onto both sides of meat. Remove unrendered fat from skillet, add steaks and sear 1 minute on each side. Reduce heat and continue cooking, allowing 6 minutes on each side for rare and 10 minutes per side for medium. Transfer meat to heated serving plates and keep warm while preparing sauce.

Pour off excess fat in skillet. Deglaze pan by adding wine and Cognac. Blend in Glace de Viande and cook over high heat until sauce thickens. Slice steaks, pour sauce over and serve immediately.

Glace de Viande

5 pounds veal bones, cracked
2 pounds chicken necks and backs
3 carrots
2 large onions, unpeeled and cut
  into quarters
2 celery stalks (including leaves),
  cut coarsely
3 garlic cloves, unpeeled and
  crushed
2 bay leaves
2 teaspoons salt

1 teaspoon crushed black
  peppercorns
  Pinch of dried thyme

¾ cup all purpose flour

2 cups dry red wine
12 cups beef stock
2 cups tomato puree
2 leeks (including green part), cut
  coarsely
3 Italian flat-leaf parsley sprigs

Preheat oven to 475°F. Combine bones, chicken parts, carrots, onions, celery, garlic, bay leaves, salt, peppercorns and thyme in large shallow roasting pan and roast uncovered for 50 minutes.

Remove pan from oven. Sprinkle flour over bones and stir to mix evenly. Return to oven and continue roasting 15 to 20 minutes. Transfer to stockpot.

Set roasting pan over medium heat. Add wine and cook, scraping bottom and sides of pan to loosen browned particles. Add to stockpot along with remaining ingredients. Bring to boil, skimming off foam as it accumulates, then reduce heat and simmer 3 to 4 hours, adding more stock or water if necessary. Skim off all fat. Remove bones; carefully strain into another large pot. Continue simmering until reduced to consistency of whipping cream. Store in refrigerator or freezer.

Filet Mignon with Mushrooms and Prosciutto

4 servings

¼ cup (½ stick) butter
4 1-inch-thick filets mignons
4 tablespoons (¼ cup) Cognac
4 ⅛-inch-thick slices pâté de foie gras
4 thin slices truffle (optional)

4 mushrooms, coarsely chopped
4 slices prosciutto
½ cup whipping cream
Worcestershire sauce
Salt and freshly ground pepper

Melt butter in large skillet over high heat. Add beef and sear quickly on each side. Reduce heat to medium and baste both sides of each filet mignon with 1 tablespoon Cognac. Top each with slice of pâté (spreading evenly to edges), truffle slice, mushrooms and prosciutto. Transfer meat to heated platter using slotted spoon. Blend ½ cup cream and Worcestershire sauce to taste into pan juices. Reduce heat to low and cook 10 minutes. Season with salt and pepper. Return meat to pan and baste with sauce. Cover and cook 5 minutes. Return filets mignons to platter, spoon sauce over and serve.

Kohlrabi Sautéed with Beef

Peppers and preserved kohlrabi give this dish its spice. Remaining kohlrabi will keep for several months.

2 main-course servings or 4 servings as part of multi-course Chinese meal

7 ounces beef flank steak
¼ cup water
1 tablespoon dark soy sauce
¼ teaspoon cornstarch

3 large fresh red chilies
2 fresh jalapeño *or* other green chilies
2½ pieces pressed bean curd*

2½ ounces canned preserved kohlrabi, Szechwan preserved kohlrabi *or* Szechwan preserved vegetable*

2 tablespoons vegetable oil

Thinly slice beef; cut slices into ⅒ × 1-inch shreds. Mix in small bowl with water, soy sauce and cornstarch. Marinate at least 30 minutes.

Remove veins and seeds from chilies. Cut into ⅒ × 1-inch strips. Rinse bean curd and pat dry. Cut into ⅒ × 1-inch strips. Rinse chili powder from kohlrabi. Cut into ⅒ × 1-inch strips.

Heat wok or heavy large skillet over high heat 1 minute. Pour in 1 tablespoon oil and heat 30 seconds. Add chilies and stir 2 minutes. Add bean curd and kohlrabi and toss 1 minute. Transfer to bowl. Wash wok and wipe dry. Set over high heat 1 minute. Add 1 tablespoon oil and heat 30 seconds. Add beef mixture and stir-fry until no longer pink, about 1½ minutes. Add chilies and bean curd and toss (if meat sticks, add 1 tablespoon water). Transfer to platter. Serve immediately.

*Available in oriental markets.

Fortune Garden Orange Beef

Flash-freeze meat first for easier slicing.

4 to 8 servings

1½ pounds beef flank steak, sliced into ¼-inch-thick strips
⅔ cup plus 3 tablespoons water
½ teaspoon baking soda

3 tablespoons dry Sherry
1 egg white
3½ tablespoons cornstarch
2 tablespoons vegetable oil

2 green onions, cut into ½-inch lengths (about ⅓ cup)
3 tablespoons dried orange peel*
3 thin slices fresh ginger, chopped
1 long, thin fresh hot red chili, chopped (optional)

¼ cup chicken stock
3 tablespoons light soy sauce
2 tablespoons sugar
1 teaspoon sesame oil**

4 cups vegetable oil

10 small dried hot red chilies, or to taste

Place beef in bowl. Combine ⅔ cup water with baking soda and pour over beef. Refrigerate at least 1 hour or overnight.

Rinse beef thoroughly under cold running water. Drain well and pat dry. Transfer to dry bowl. Add 1 tablespoon wine and egg white and stir briskly, using circular motion, until egg white is foamy. Add 1½ tablespoons cornstarch and 2 tablespoons oil.

Combine green onions, orange peel, ginger and chili in small bowl.

Combine remaining 2 tablespoons cornstarch and remaining 3 tablespoons water in small bowl. Add remaining 2 tablespoons wine. Blend in chicken stock, soy sauce, sugar and sesame oil.

Heat 4 cups oil in wok or heavy large skillet over high heat until almost smoking. Add beef and cook about 45 seconds, stirring constantly. Remove beef with slotted spoon and drain (do not turn off heat). Return meat to wok and cook 15 seconds, stirring. Drain again. Return meat to wok and cook 15 seconds, stirring. Drain well. (Repeated cooking will make meat crisp outside while remaining juicy inside.)

Drain all but 2 tablespoons oil from wok. Return wok to high heat and add hot chilies, stirring until almost black, about 30 seconds. Remove chilies with slotted spoon and discard. Add green onion mixture to wok and stir briefly. Add beef and cook, stirring constantly, about 10 seconds. Add wine mixture and stir until meat is well coated and piping hot, about 15 seconds. Turn into dish and serve immediately.

*For dried orange peel, remove peel of 1 orange, scraping all white pith from inside. Cut peel into 1-inch squares. Arrange on baking sheet. Let stand in warm place until peel is thoroughly dried, about 24 hours. Store in tightly covered container.
**Available in oriental markets.

Beef-Cauliflower Stir-fry

4 servings

2 tablespoons (¼ stick) butter
1 pound beef flank *or* rib steak, sliced to ⅓-inch thickness and cut into ½-inch dice
1 green bell pepper, cored, seeded and cut into ¾-inch dice
4 cups cauliflower florets
¼ cup soy sauce

1 garlic clove, minced
1½ cups beef stock
2 tablespoons cornstarch
½ teaspoon sugar (optional)
1 cup sliced green onion (about 4 large)
Freshly cooked rice

Melt butter in wok or heavy large skillet over medium-high heat. Add meat and green pepper and stir-fry until meat is browned, about 1 to 2 minutes. Remove meat and pepper from wok and set aside. Add cauliflower, soy sauce and garlic, stirring gently. Cover and simmer until cauliflower is crisp-tender, about 5 to 7 minutes. Combine stock, cornstarch and sugar in small bowl. Add stock mixture and green onion to wok and stir until sauce is thickened. Return beef and pepper to wok, tossing gently. Serve immediately over rice.

Chinese Pepper Steak

4 servings

1 1½- to 2-pound beef flank steak, trimmed
3 tablespoons soy sauce
1 tablespoon dry Sherry *or* rice wine
2 teaspoons cornstarch
1 teaspoon sugar

4 tablespoons peanut *or* vegetable oil
1 medium-size green bell pepper, cut into ½-inch dice
4 ⅛-inch slices peeled fresh ginger *or* ¼ teaspoon ground ginger
Freshly cooked rice

Cut meat lengthwise into thirds and then crosswise into ¼-inch strips. Combine soy sauce, Sherry, cornstarch and sugar in medium bowl. Add meat, turning to coat. Cover and marinate in refrigerator 30 minutes.

Heat wok or skillet over medium-high heat. Pour in 1 tablespoon oil and swirl to coat. Add pepper and stir-fry until crisp-tender, about 3 minutes. Transfer to dish. Pour remaining oil into wok and heat over medium-high heat. Add ginger and stir-fry briefly. Add steak with marinade and stir-fry until meat is lightly browned and marinade is reduced, about 2 minutes. Discard fresh ginger. Return pepper to wok and stir-fry until heated through, about 1 minute. Serve over rice.

Beef in Creamy Paprika Sauce

Serve over buttered noodles tossed with poppy seed or on a bed of rice.

2 servings

½ pound thinly sliced beef chuck, cut into ½-inch strips
All purpose flour
2 tablespoons (¼ stick) butter
1 tablespoon vegetable oil

½ cup chopped onion
1 cup whipping cream
1 tablespoon tomato paste
2 teaspoons paprika
Salt and freshly ground pepper

Dust beef strips lightly with flour, shaking off excess. Heat butter and oil in medium skillet over medium-high heat. Add beef and stir-fry until brown on all sides. Remove from pan; set aside.

Reduce heat to low. Add onion and sauté until golden. Stir in cream, tomato paste and paprika, blending well. Increase heat to medium and simmer sauce, stirring constantly, until thickened. Return beef to skillet and heat through. Season to taste with salt and pepper. Serve immediately.

🍂 *Roasting and Baking*

Peppered Rib Eye of Beef

8 to 10 servings

1 5-pound rib eye of beef roast, trimmed
½ cup whole black peppercorns, coarsely ground
½ teaspoon ground cardamom
1 tablespoon tomato paste

1 teaspoon paprika
½ teaspoon garlic powder
1 cup soy sauce
¾ cup red wine vinegar

1 cup water

Place beef in 9 × 13-inch baking dish. Combine ground peppercorns and cardamom seed in small bowl. Firmly press pepper mixture into beef. Combine tomato paste, paprika and garlic powder in medium bowl. Stir in soy sauce and vinegar. Pour marinade over beef. Cover and refrigerate at least 6 hours, or overnight, basting occasionally.

Remove beef from refrigerator. Let stand in marinade at room temperature about 1 hour.

Preheat oven to 300°F. Remove beef from marinade using tongs and wrap in heavy-duty foil. Discard marinade. Transfer beef to shallow pan. Roast to desired doneness, about 2 hours for medium rare.

Remove beef from baking pan. Degrease drippings. Combine 1 cup drippings with 1 cup water in small saucepan. Bring sauce to boil over medium-high heat. Unwrap beef and transfer to large platter. Slice and serve immediately, serving sauce separately.

Standing Rib Roast of Beef with Madeira Sauce

10 servings

2 teaspoons salt
1 teaspoon dried thyme
1 teaspoon freshly ground pepper
1 10-pound standing rib of beef (4 ribs), trimmed, fat scored, chine removed and tied onto roast

Sauce
⅔ cup water
1½ tablespoons butter
Juice of ½ lemon

¼ teaspoon salt
½ pound small white mushrooms, trimmed (sliced or halved if desired)

¼ cup (½ stick) butter
½ cup minced shallot
1 cup beef stock
½ cup Madeira
1 tablespoon tomato paste
Salt and freshly ground pepper

Combine salt, thyme and pepper in small bowl and blend well. Rub into roast, covering entire surface. Transfer meat to rack in large roasting pan. Let stand at room temperature 1 hour until ready to use.

For sauce: Combine water, butter, lemon juice and salt in nonaluminum medium saucepan and bring to boil over medium-high heat. Reduce heat to low and stir in mushrooms. Cover and cook gently about 5 minutes. Uncover and set aside. *(Can be prepared several hours ahead to this point. Let stand at room temperature until ready to use.)*

Preheat oven to 500°F. Roast meat 10 minutes. Reduce oven temperature to 350°F and continue roasting until meat thermometer inserted in thickest portion of meat without touching bone registers desired degree of doneness, about 130°F for rare (about 17 minutes per pound); do not baste. Transfer roast to heated serving platter. Tent with foil and keep warm.

Discard as much fat as possible from roasting pan. Add ¼ cup butter to pan and melt over medium-high heat. Stir in shallot and sauté until tender. Drain mushroom cooking liquid into measuring cup and add water, if necessary, to equal 1 cup. Pour into roasting pan with beef stock, Madeira and tomato paste and blend well. Reduce heat to low and cook, stirring up any browned bits, until liquid is reduced to 2 cups. Stir in mushrooms and cook just until heated through. Season with salt and pepper to taste. Transfer to heated sauceboat. Carve roast at table and serve immediately with sauce.

Roast Beef and Yorkshire Pudding for Two

The meat must be thoroughly frozen to cook properly, so be sure to buy it several days ahead to wrap and freeze.

2 servings

1 rib of a standing rib roast (about 2½ pounds), frozen

½ cup milk
½ cup all purpose flour
1 egg

¼ teaspoon salt

2 tablespoons (6 teaspoons) drippings from roast beef
Horseradish Cream Sauce (see following recipe)

Preheat oven to 400°F. Place meat in roasting pan, fat side up, balanced on the bone. Roast until meat thermometer inserted in thickest part of meat without touching bone registers desired degree of doneness, about 140°F for rare (about 1½ hours), 160°F for medium (1 hour and 40 minutes) and 170°F for well done (1 hour and 50 minutes).

Meanwhile, combine milk, flour, egg and salt in blender or processor and mix well. Cover and refrigerate 1 hour.

Spoon 1½ teaspoons drippings into each of 4 custard cups. Divide batter evenly among cups. Bake with meat during last 20 minutes of roasting time, then remove meat from oven and tent with foil to keep warm. Reduce oven temperature to 350°F and continue baking pudding until puffed and golden, about 10 to 15 minutes. Carve roast at table. Serve with pudding and Horseradish Cream Sauce.

Horseradish Cream Sauce

Makes about ½ cup

2 tablespoons prepared horseradish
1 teaspoon tarragon wine vinegar
½ teaspoon sugar
½ teaspoon dry mustard

¼ cup whipping cream, softly whipped
Salt and freshly ground pepper

Combine first 4 ingredients in small bowl and blend well. Fold in whipped cream. Taste and season with salt and pepper. Refrigerate before serving.

Brisket with Prunes

*Fresh, hot buttered noodles
and a crisp green salad
with toasted almonds are
perfect partners for this
tasty dish.*

4 to 6 servings

2 onions, sliced
1 2- to 3-pound lean beef brisket

1 12-ounce can beer, or more
1 cup dried pitted prunes
1 cup dried apricots
3 tablespoons firmly packed brown
   sugar
2 tablespoons orange marmalade
   (preferably bitter)

1 tablespoon brandy
1 tablespoon grated lemon peel
   Juice of 1 lemon
¾ teaspoon ground ginger
½ teaspoon cinnamon
½ teaspoon Worcestershire sauce
½ teaspoon freshly ground pepper

Preheat oven to 350°F. Cut piece of aluminum foil large enough to wrap brisket. Sprinkle half of sliced onions over foil in layer about same size as brisket. Set brisket over onions. Sprinkle remaining onions over top. Seal tightly. Set in large shallow pan. Roast 3 hours.

Combine 12 ounces beer with remaining ingredients in large saucepan and bring to boil over medium-high heat. Remove from heat. Discard foil and spread fruit mixture over brisket. Reduce oven temperature to 300°F. Cover pan and continue roasting 1 hour, adding more beer to pan if sauce appears dry. Transfer brisket to heated platter. Surround with fruit and sauce.

Beef Sorrentine

2 servings

2 tablespoons olive oil
1 14-ounce prime filet mignon,
   trimmed
1½ tablespoons clarified butter
½ teaspoon all purpose flour
½ teaspoon finely chopped onion
½ cup chicken *or* beef stock

3 tablespoons dry Marsala
   Minced fresh parsley
   Freshly ground pepper
1 ⅛-inch-thick slice eggplant,
   lightly sautéed
1 slice prosciutto
1 thin slice mozzarella

Preheat oven to 550°F. Heat oil in heavy medium skillet over high heat. Add beef and brown on all sides, about 9 minutes. Remove beef. Heat clarified butter in another heavy medium skillet over low heat. Stir in flour and onion. Add beef to skillet and turn in butter. Add stock and Marsala. Turn beef in liquid. Sprinkle with parsley and pepper. Top with eggplant, prosciutto and mozzarella. Baste beef with liquid in skillet. Transfer to baking dish. Bake about 5 minutes. Slice and serve immediately.

Meat Loaf with Three Cheeses

12 servings

Butter (for pan)
Breadcrumbs (for pan)

2 pounds ground beef
1 large onion, finely chopped
1 garlic clove, finely chopped
2 cups fresh spinach (stems discarded), washed, dried and finely chopped
½ cup freshly grated Parmesan cheese
2 tablespoons finely chopped fresh parsley *or* 1 teaspoon dried

2 eggs, lightly beaten
3 slices French, Italian *or* homemade white bread, soaked in ½ cup milk 5 minutes, drained and squeezed dry
2 teaspoons salt
Freshly ground pepper

1 cup finely cubed mozzarella cheese
1 cup slivered Gruyère cheese
Breadcrumbs
Butter

Generously butter 12 × 4 × 2½-inch baking pan. Sprinkle with breadcrumbs, shaking out excess.

Combine meat, onion, garlic, spinach, Parmesan, parsley, eggs, bread, salt and pepper in large bowl and blend well.

Preheat oven to 350°F. Divide mixture into 3 portions. Pat ⅓ of mixture into bottom of prepared pan (be sure meat touches sides of pan). Sprinkle mozzarella cubes over top. Add another ⅓ meat mixture and cover with Gruyère slivers. Add remaining ⅓ meat mixture, patting in place to edge of pan. Sprinkle with breadcrumbs and dot with butter. Bake until cooked through, about 1 hour. Remove from pan using large spatula. Transfer to large platter. Serve hot or cold.

Beef-Mushroom Turnovers (Pirozhki)

Freeze any remaining turnovers to reheat for another meal.

Makes 8 to 10 turnovers

Pastry
½ cup all purpose flour
   Pinch of salt
3½ tablespoons unsalted butter, well chilled
4 teaspoons (scant) ice water

Beef-Mushroom Filling
1¼ teaspoons butter

⅓ cup minced mushrooms (1 ounce)
¼ cup minced onion
4 ounces lean ground beef
1 tablespoon minced fresh dill *or* 1 teaspoon dried dillweed
   Salt and freshly ground pepper
1 egg, beaten to blend

For pastry: Combine flour and salt in medium bowl. Cut in butter until mixture resembles coarse meal. Sprinkle with ice water and blend until pastry forms ball. Cover and chill.

For beef-mushroom filling: Melt butter in medium skillet over medium-low heat. Add mushrooms and onion and cook until onion is soft and translucent, about 5 minutes. Add beef, increase heat to medium high and cook, breaking up meat with fork, until no trace of pink remains. Stir in dill and seasoning. Blend in 1 tablespoon egg, reserving remainder for brushing pastries.

Roll dough out on lightly floured surface to thickness of ⅛ inch. Cut as many circles as possible from dough using 3- to 3½-inch cutter. Reroll scraps and cut additional circles. Spoon about 1 teaspoon filling onto center of each circle. Brush edges of dough lightly with beaten egg. Fold dough over filling to form half-circles; press edges together firmly to seal. Arrange on baking sheet. Brush with remaining egg. Chill 1 hour.

Preheat oven to 350°F. Bake until golden brown, about 20 to 25 minutes. Serve turnovers warm.

Steak and Kidney Pie

Bottom round or chuck will give the best flavor to this dish and will not fall apart during long cooking.

Complete the meal with a green salad and a cooling custard for dessert.

2 servings

¾ pound bottom round *or* beef stew meat, cut into bite-size pieces
4 lamb kidneys, trimmed and cut into cubes
3 tablespoons all purpose flour
4 tablespoons vegetable oil
1 onion, sliced
2 ounces mushrooms, sliced
1 cup beef stock
1 cup red wine
2 tablespoons minced fresh parsley

1 tablespoon fresh lemon juice
1 tablespoon tomato paste
1 tablespoon Worcestershire sauce
½ teaspoon dried thyme
   Freshly ground pepper

Basic Pastry Crust (see following recipe)

1 egg yolk beaten with 1 tablespoon water

Dredge beef and kidneys in flour, shaking off excess. Heat 3 tablespoons oil in Dutch oven over high heat. Add beef and kidneys (in batches if necessary; *do not crowd*) and brown on all sides. Remove from pan. Add remaining oil to same pan with onion and mushrooms and sauté until onion is lightly browned, about 5 minutes. Return beef and kidneys to pan. Blend in remaining ingredients. Cover and simmer over medium-low heat until meat is tender, about 2 hours, stirring occasionally. Using slotted spoon, remove meat, onion and mushrooms from pan and set aside. Increase heat to high and cook until sauce is reduced to 1 cup, about 8 minutes. Return beef and kidneys to sauce. Refrigerate overnight.

Roll chilled pastry out between sheets of waxed paper. Cut into 2 circles slightly larger in diameter than two 1½-cup ramekins or soufflé dishes. Brush rims of dishes and edges of pastry circles with cold water. Divide steak and kidney filling between dishes; *filling must be well chilled or underside of pastry will be soggy.* Drape pastry over dishes, crimping to seal and trimming any excess. Cut small hole in center of each crust to allow steam to escape.

Preheat oven to 450°F. For final professional touch, use excess pastry to decorate tops of pies with roses, tassels or leaves. Roll scraps out between sheets of waxed paper.

To make rose, cut ½ × 4-inch strip of dough. Wind strip around itself, starting with tightly wrapped center and making spiral looser as you wind. Open up outside "petals." Cut thin strand of pastry to make stem. To make tassel, cut 1 × 3-inch strip of dough. Make cuts across ⅔ of width of strip to form fringe. Roll up lengthwise, pinching base together and opening fringed end of tassel. To make leaf, use small scrap of dough and trace leaf or freehand imitation, making veins with small sharp knife. Several leaves can be arranged around hole in crust to form pretty design.

Brush pastry with egg yolk mixture. Bake pies 10 minutes. Reduce oven temperature to 375°F and continue baking until pastry is golden brown, 15 to 20 minutes. Serve immediately.

Basic Pastry Crust

For the flakiest pastry crust use the minimum amount of water.

1 cup all purpose flour *or* ½ cup all purpose flour and ½ cup whole wheat flour
½ teaspoon salt
½ teaspoon celery, fennel *or* poppy seed (optional)
¼ cup grated sharp cheddar cheese (optional)
2 teaspoons toasted sesame seed (toast 10 minutes at 350°F) (optional)

1 teaspoon grated lemon peel (optional)
¼ cup lard
¼ cup (½ stick) butter
2 to 3 tablespoons ice water

Mix flour and salt in large bowl. Add one of the optional flavorings if desired.

Cut lard and butter into flour mixture using pastry blender or 2 knives until mixture resembles coarse meal. Sprinkle in water a little at a time, mixing until dough begins to cling together. Wrap dough tightly in plastic and refrigerate at least 1 hour or overnight.

❧ *Braising and Poaching*

Classic Pot Roast

This pot roast is a family or party dish with a decidedly French touch. Using pig's feet is an old trick for giving body and character to robust sauces because of its wealth of natural gelatin. For best results, marinate the meat for 1 to 2 days. Serve with a Côtes du Rhône or a full-bodied California Zinfandel.

8 to 10 servings

Marinade
- 4 cups dry red wine
- ¼ cup wine vinegar
- 3 tablespoons olive oil
- 1 medium onion, chopped
- 2 garlic cloves, crushed
- 2 bay leaves
- 1 3-inch strip orange peel
- 6 whole cloves
- ½ teaspoon fennel seed, crushed
- ½ teaspoon ground ginger
- ½ teaspoon dried thyme
- ½ teaspoon dried savory
- ¼ teaspoon freshly ground pepper

- 1 6- to 7-pound beef bottom *or* top round roast

- ¼ cup clarified unsalted butter

- 2 large onions, minced
- 2 large carrots, minced
- 1 celery stalk, minced
- 2 fresh (not pickled) pig's feet (optional)
- 3 cups beef stock
- 2 tablespoons tomato paste
  Salt and freshly ground pepper

- 1 pound carrots, cut into large dice (2 cups diced)
- 1 pound small baking onions, peeled (about 32)
- 1 pound rutabaga, peeled and cut into large dice
- 1 pound green beans, trimmed and cut into 1-inch pieces

For marinade: Combine first 13 ingredients in nonaluminum bowl just large enough to hold roast. Blend well.

Add meat, turning to coat all sides. Cover with plastic wrap and refrigerate 1 to 2 days, turning once a day. (Marinating can be omitted: Combine first 13 ingredients in large saucepan and boil 10 minutes. Set wine mixture aside for braising the roast.)

Drain meat, reserving marinade. Pat meat dry. Strain marinade through fine sieve, pressing on vegetables with back of spoon to extract liquid; set aside for braising roast. Heat clarified butter in 5- to 6-quart Dutch oven or flameproof baking dish over medium-high heat. Add meat and brown on all sides, turning with spatula to avoid piercing. Set meat aside. Drain all but about 2 tablespoons fat from pan. Return to medium-high heat. Add minced onions, carrots, and celery and cook until golden brown, 9 to 10 minutes. Add pig's feet, beef stock, tomato paste, salt and pepper and reserved marinade and bring to simmer. Return meat to pan. Reduce heat to low, cover tightly and simmer gently until meat is barely tender, 2 to 2½ hours.

Stir in diced carrots, baking onions and rutabaga. Cover and cook 15 minutes. Add green beans and continue cooking 20 minutes. Remove from heat, uncover and let cool. Discard pig's feet. Refrigerate at least 1 day, preferably 2 days.

To serve, degrease braising liquid. Place pan over low heat and gently reheat meat and liquid 1 hour. Slice about ⅔ of roast and arrange slices with remaining roast on heated platter. Remove vegetables from sauce using slotted spoon and arrange around meat. Taste sauce and reduce to desired concentration of flavor. Spoon some sauce over meat and serve. Serve remaining sauce separately.

Sweet and Tangy Beef and Vegetables

4 to 6 servings

2 tablespoons vegetable oil
2 pounds beef stew meat, cut into 1-inch pieces
1 large green bell pepper, cored, seeded and cut into 1-inch dice
1 large onion, thinly sliced
½ cup vinegar

2 cups thinly sliced carrot
2 8-ounce cans tomato sauce
½ cup light molasses
2 teaspoons chili powder
1 teaspoon paprika
1 teaspoon salt
Freshly cooked rice

Heat oil in heavy large skillet over medium-high heat. Add meat and brown on all sides. Transfer to slow cooker. Add green pepper and onion to same skillet. Cover, reduce heat to low and cook 10 minutes. Add to meat. Pour vinegar into skillet and stir, scraping up any browned bits. Turn mixture into slow cooker. Add carrot, tomato sauce, molasses, chili powder, paprika and salt. Cover and cook on Low for 6 to 7 hours or on High for 4 hours. Serve hot with rice.

Bistecca Pizzaiola

This authentic Italian family recipe is served at Julie's Ristorante in Ogunquit, Maine.

Wrap meat securely and flash-freeze for 30 minutes to facilitate slicing.

3 to 4 servings

½ cup olive oil
¼ cup (½ stick) butter
1½ pounds top round, trimmed and cut crosswise into very thin strips (about 3 × 1½ inches)
½ pound mushrooms, sliced
½ large onion, thinly sliced
2 garlic cloves, thinly sliced
5 Italian plum tomatoes, chopped, *or 5 ounces canned Italian plum tomatoes*

½ cup fresh parsley leaves (preferably Italian flat-leaf)
½ teaspoon dried oregano
Salt and freshly ground pepper
1 cup dry red wine
½ cup freshly grated Parmesan cheese

Heat oil and butter in heavy large skillet over medium-high heat. Add meat and brown quickly on all sides. Transfer to large platter. Add mushrooms to skillet and sauté until edges are browned, about 3 to 5 minutes. Remove with slotted spoon and place over meat. Add onion and garlic to skillet and sauté until onion is lightly browned, about 3 to 5 minutes. Add tomatoes and mash slightly with fork. Stir in parsley and oregano. Season to taste with salt and pepper. Reduce heat and simmer 30 minutes. Stir in wine and cheese and simmer 15 minutes. Return meat and mushrooms to skillet, cover and simmer 1 hour, stirring occasionally and adding more wine (or water) as necessary if mixture is too dry.

Esterhazy Rostbraten

This delicious, hearty roast is named after one of the leading aristocratic families of the Austro-Hungarian Empire. It is very simple to prepare and is an excellent dinner party dish.

4 servings

2 medium onions, finely chopped
½ cup toasted breadcrumbs
¼ cup minced cooked bacon
1 teaspoon capers, rinsed and drained
½ teaspoon chopped fresh parsley
1 1½-pound beef fillet (1½ inches thick)
4 tablespoons (½ stick) butter

2 large carrots, chopped
1 large parsnip, chopped
1 celery stalk, chopped
½ teaspoon all purpose flour
½ cup whipping cream
½ teaspoon medium-hot paprika
Salt and freshly ground pepper
¼ cup imported Madeira

🍒 Braising

Braising is a cooking method commonly used for the preparation of the less tender cuts of beef, such as chuck, round or shoulder. This method—also known as pot roasting—calls for the meat to be slowly browned first (to concentrate juices at the center of the roast and to give color and flavor to the sauce) and then slowly simmered, usually in a small amount of liquid. The process is a simple one, but the perfect pot roast—one that is tender and flavorful and accompanied by a rich-tasting sauce—demands a little attention.

Variations

Daube: French method of braising without first browning the meat. Usually refers to a meat that is marinated and then cooked in its own marinade.

Etuvée: French method of braising in butter, but with little or no liquid. The meat is cooked in a very low oven or over hot, but not boiling, water. This causes the food to slowly exude moisture, making the addition of liquid unnecessary. Usually used to cook vegetables or stews with thick sauces that have a tendency to scorch.

Poêlage: Refers to meat that is cooked in a covered pan in a low oven with butter or other fat.

Stewing: Refers to meat cut into cubes and braised on top of the stove.

Great Hints

- To facilitate slicing meat and defatting sauce, prepare pot roast 1 day before serving and chill overnight.
- Like soups, braised or stewed meats improve in flavor when they are reheated; they also freeze beautifully.
- It is important to use the right pot. It should have a heavy bottom and be just big enough to contain meat and vegetables. There should not be a wide space between meat and lid.
- When lifting the pot lid, do it quickly, inverting it to prevent condensation from dripping into sauce.
- Commercial stocks are usually saltier than homemade varieties. Dilute with wine, beer or tomato juice.
- Do not add salt to braised foods. In most cases, the concentration of pan juices provides sufficient flavoring.

Combine half of chopped onions, breadcrumbs, bacon, capers and parsley in large bowl and mix well. Cut deep horizontal pocket in beef fillet and fill with onion mixture. Melt 2 tablespoons butter in large skillet over medium-high heat. Add fillet and sear on both sides. Transfer to Dutch oven using tongs; reserve drippings.

Melt remaining 2 tablespoons butter in another large skillet over medium heat. Add remaining onion, carrots, parsnip and celery and sauté 2 to 3 minutes. Push vegetables to side of skillet. Add flour and reserved drippings. Gradually stir in cream, mixing until smooth. Stir in vegetables from side of skillet. Add paprika and season with salt and pepper to taste. Pour sauce over fillet. Cover and simmer over medium-low heat until tender, basting occasionally, about 30 minutes. Stir in Madeira and cook 5 more minutes. Serve immediately.

Flemish Beef Stew

A takeoff on the famous Belgian carbonnade flamande *that uses the local beer for its special quality. Porter or stout most closely approximates the aged, robust brew traditionally used.*

This recipe can be doubled easily and freezes well. Pork shoulder can be substituted for beef; for another variation, add about 8 ounces of pitted prunes to stew along with the bread and mustard (although the Belgians would scoff at this untraditional idea). Serve with boiled potatoes, green salad and, of course, beer.

4 servings

2 ounces salt pork, coarsely chopped
1 to 1½ pounds beef chuck, trimmed of excess fat and cut into chunks
3 large onions, thinly sliced (about 1½ pounds)
1 teaspoon all purpose flour
2 cups stout *or* porter (do not use lager or Pilsner)
1½ to 2 tablespoons vinegar
1 tablespoon firmly packed brown sugar

1 parsley sprig
1 bay leaf
1 branch fresh thyme *or* 1 teaspoon dried

2½ to 3 tablespoons Dijon *or* German mustard
1 large slice stale French bread (about 5 × 3 × ½ inches)
Salt and freshly ground pepper

Blanch salt pork in boiling water 5 minutes. Drain and rinse well; pat dry. Transfer to heavy nonaluminum large skillet and cook over medium heat until lightly browned. Remove from skillet using slotted spoon and reserve for use in salads or other dishes. Increase heat to medium high. Add beef to skillet in batches (*do not crowd*) and cook until well browned on all sides, turning with spatula. Transfer meat to heavy nonaluminum 2- to 3-quart saucepan. Add onions to skillet, reduce heat slightly and cook until deep golden brown, about 10 minutes, stirring occasionally. Blend in flour and cook about 30 seconds, watching carefully so flour does not burn. Add stout and stir, scraping up any browned bits. Bring mixture to boil. Pour over beef. Blend in vinegar, sugar, parsley, bay leaf and thyme. Cover saucepan and simmer mixture for 30 minutes.

Spread mustard over bread. Press bread into stew. Cover and cook until meat is tender, about 1 hour. Remove bay leaf and discard. Taste and adjust seasoning. Serve immediately.

Pichelsteiner One-pot (Pichelsteiner Eintopf)

A German-style meat stew. Very good made 1 day ahead and reheated.

4 to 5 servings

2 tablespoons (¼ stick) butter
2 tablespoons vegetable oil
1½ pounds beef rump *or* ¾ pound beef rump and ¾ pound pork shoulder, trimmed, cut into 1-inch cubes and patted dry
1 medium onion, chopped
⅓ cup chopped fresh parsley
1 tablespoon finely chopped celery root
1 cup beef stock
1 medium tomato, peeled, cored, seeded and chopped

1 teaspoon imported sweet paprika
⅓ teaspoon salt
¼ teaspoon freshly ground pepper
4 medium potatoes, peeled and coarsely cubed
3 medium carrots, coarsely sliced
2 medium turnips, peeled and coarsely cubed
1 cup fresh green beans, trimmed and broken into 2- to 3-inch pieces
2 tablespoons snipped fresh chives (garnish)

Melt butter with oil in large Dutch oven or flameproof casserole over high heat. Add meat in batches (*do not crowd*) and brown on all sides. Remove with slotted spoon and set aside. Reduce heat to medium, add onion, parsley and celery root and cook, stirring constantly, 4 to 5 minutes. Blend in beef stock, tomato, paprika, salt and pepper. Return meat to Dutch oven. Top with layers of potatoes, carrots, turnips and green beans. Reduce heat to low, cover and cook until meat is tender, about 60 to 70 minutes. Adjust seasoning. Transfer to soup tureen or serve from Dutch oven. Garnish with snipped chives.

Poires en robes de chambre

Veal Chops with
Capers and Cream

Veal Chops en Papillote with Leeks,
Carrots, Parsnips and Spiced Butter

Pot-au-feu

Steak with Bleu Cheese and Mustard Sauce

Irwin Horowitz

*Moroccan Lamb Tajine
with Dates*

Stuffed Leg of Lamb Wrapped in Pastry

Vegetable-stuffed Beef Roll with Tomato Sauce (Morcón)

The beef is presented sliced, showing off the spiral pattern of the stuffing.

12 servings

1 3-pound eye of round beef roast

  Freshly ground pepper
1 ⅓-pound piece slab bacon
4 Chinese sausages, halved lengthwise
3 large carrots, peeled and cut into thirds lengthwise
2 hard-cooked eggs, quartered lengthwise
1 large green bell pepper, cut into ⅓-inch strips
1 large red bell pepper, cut into ⅓-inch strips
16 pimiento-stuffed green olives

Sauce
  2 cups water
  2 cups tomato sauce
  2 medium onions, finely chopped
  ½ cup distilled vinegar
  2 bay leaves
  ¼ teaspoon salt
  ¼ teaspoon freshly ground pepper

  Vegetable oil (for frying)

To cut beef into 1 long flat piece, insert sharp long knife ¾ inch above work surface. Cut along bottom of meat down full length parallel to work surface, leaving ¾-inch "hinge" at far long side. Pull back on top of roast to uncover cut strip of meat. Insert knife where strip attaches to roast and repeat. Continue cutting until roast is opened into 1 long strip. Pound meat strip to ½-inch thickness.

Sprinkle meat with pepper. Slice slab bacon lengthwise into 4 strips, then halve lengthwise. Arrange bacon, sausages, carrots, eggs, bell peppers and olives crosswise atop meat in alternating rows. Roll meat up tightly, starting at short end. Tie roulade securely at 2-inch intervals, using kitchen twine.

For sauce: Combine all remaining ingredients except vegetable oil in heavy medium saucepan and bring to boil. Reduce heat and simmer 3 minutes.

Preheat oven to 350°F. Heat ½ inch of oil in deep heavy large skillet over medium-high heat. Pat roulade dry and brown on all sides. Transfer to deep roasting pan. Pour tomato sauce over meat. Cover tightly with foil. Bake until meat is tender, about 2 hours, basting with sauce every 20 minutes.

Set roulade on platter; reserve sauce. Let meat cool. Cover and refrigerate until chilled. *(Can be prepared 1 day ahead to this point and refrigerated.)*

Preheat oven to 350°F. Cut roulade into ¾-inch slices across grain. Arrange cut side down in single layer in large roasting pan. Bake just until warm, about 15 minutes. Reheat sauce. Remove bay leaves and discard. Spoon sauce onto warm serving platter. Top with meat and serve immediately.

Mexican Beef Fillet with Tomato-Orange Cumin Sauce

The bonus of this recipe is the beef poaching liquid, which can be served as a soup. Strain before using.

6 servings

1 teaspoon olive oil
3 medium garlic cloves, minced
1 teaspoon ground cumin
½ teaspoon ground coriander
¼ teaspoon dried red pepper flakes
2 cups chicken *or* beef stock, or more
1 cup water, or more

1 teaspoon vinegar
1 bay leaf
¾ teaspoon coarse salt
1 2½-pound center cut fillet of beef tenderloin, trimmed of all fat, tied lengthwise and crosswise
Tomato-Orange Cumin Sauce (see following recipe)

Heat oil in heavy Dutch oven (wide enough just to hold fillet) over high heat. Add garlic, cumin, coriander and pepper flakes and stir 30 seconds. Add 2 cups stock, 1 cup water, vinegar, bay leaf and salt and bring to boil. Add fillet and reduce heat so liquid simmers (if meat is not covered by liquid, add more stock or water). Simmer gently 20 to 25 minutes for rare. Remove meat from pan. Let stand 5 minutes. Skim fat from surface and reserve liquid for soup, if desired. Cut meat diagonally ¼ inch thick. Spoon ⅓ cup Tomato-Orange Cumin Sauce over each serving.

Tomato-Orange Cumin Sauce

6 servings

1 cup peeled, seeded and coarsely chopped fresh tomatoes (about ¾ pound)
1 cup seeded, drained and coarsely chopped canned tomatoes (1¼ 16-ounce cans)

1 large seedless orange

1½ teaspoons olive oil
4 medium garlic cloves, minced

½ teaspoon (generous) ground cumin
¼ teaspoon ground coriander
⅛ teaspoon dried red pepper flakes
1 teaspoon tomato paste
½ teaspoon coarse salt
¼ teaspoon sugar
Freshly ground pepper
½ cup diagonally sliced green onion

Let all tomatoes drain 10 minutes.

Cut seven 2-inch strips of orange peel (orange part only). Set 4 aside. Finely chop remainder; measure ½ teaspoon and set aside. Using small, very sharp knife, remove remaining peel and all white pith from orange. To release 1 section, hold orange over bowl and cut down at slight angle on 1 side of membrane, then on other side. Repeat with remaining sections. Drain sections in small sieve over bowl. Cut each section into thirds. Set aside.

Heat oil in heavy medium skillet over high heat. Add garlic, cumin, coriander, pepper flakes and reserved strips of orange peel and stir 30 seconds. Add orange juice and cook until only glaze on bottom of pan remains, about 1 minute. Add orange sections, drained tomatoes, tomato paste, salt and sugar and cook 3 minutes, shaking pan occasionally. Discard orange peel. Season to taste with pepper. Adjust seasoning. Stir in onion and reserved chopped orange peel. Serve immediately.

❦

Pot-au-feu

2 to 3 servings

2 pounds beef chuck short ribs, cut at least 4 inches long and tied together
2 celery stalks (including leaves), cut into large pieces
1 onion, studded with 4 whole cloves
1 carrot, cut into large pieces
1 leek, cut into large pieces
1 turnip, cut into large pieces
1 bouquet garni (1 parsley sprig, 1 bay leaf, 1 garlic clove and 6 black peppercorns tied together in a cheesecloth bag)

2 carrots, cut into ½-inch slices
2 celery stalks, cut into ½-inch slices
2 leeks, cut into 1-inch pieces
1 potato, peeled and cut into ½-inch slices
½ small head cabbage, cut into large pieces
1½ teaspoons salt, or to taste

Place short ribs in 4½- to 5-quart pot. Add cold water to within 1 inch of top. Bring to boil over high heat, skimming top as necessary. Reduce heat and add next 6 ingredients. Cover and simmer until meat is fork tender, 2 to 2½ hours.

Transfer ribs to plate and set aside. Strain stock through dampened cheesecloth into large bowl. Discard vegetables and bouquet garni. Degrease stock.

Transfer ribs and stock to large saucepan. Add remaining ingredients and bring to boil. Reduce heat and simmer, stirring occasionally, until tender, about 20 minutes. Cut string from ribs and discard. Transfer ribs to platter and moisten with some of stock. Surround with vegetables and serve.

Boiled Beef in Ale

A British North Country favorite, often served with a simple horseradish sauce. The beef brisket must be marinated for at least 8 hours.

6 servings

⅓ cup apple cider vinegar
¼ cup molasses *or English treacle**
1 teaspoon dried thyme
16 peppercorns
10 whole allspice berries
6 whole cloves
3 garlic cloves, halved
2 bay leaves

1 rosemary sprig
1 large cinnamon stick
2 1-liter bottles (about) ale *or dark beer (preferably imported)
1 4- to 5-pound lean beef brisket
2 large onions, thinly sliced and rings separated

Combine vinegar, molasses, thyme, peppercorns, allspice, cloves, garlic, bay leaves, rosemary and cinnamon in large bowl. Blend in 1 cup ale. Pat brisket dry with damp cloth. Transfer to shallow large baking dish. Pour marinade over, rubbing herbs and spices onto both sides of brisket. Scatter onions over top. Cover and refrigerate at least 8 hours, turning occasionally.

Transfer brisket to stainless steel stockpot. Add marinade, onions and remaining ale. Place over medium-high heat and bring to simmer. Reduce heat, cover partially and simmer gently until fork tender, about 3 hours. Let stand in liquid until ready to serve. (If desired, strain cooking liquid through fine sieve lined with several layers of moistened cheesecloth and reduce over high heat to syrupy consistency.) Cut brisket diagonally into long thin slices. Nap slices with cooking liquid or sauce and serve.

* Available in specialty food stores.

German-style Boiled Beef (Tellerfleisch)

6 servings

2 carrots
1 onion, studded with 6 whole
   cloves
1 small celery root, quartered
1 leek (about ¾ pound), trimmed
2 teaspoons salt
10 peppercorns

10 whole allspice berries
3 garlic cloves
2 bay leaves
2 tablespoons red wine vinegar
2 tablespoons sugar
1 3-pound beef brisket

Combine all ingredients except brisket in 8- to 10-quart saucepan or Dutch oven with enough water to cover and bring to boil over high heat. Reduce heat, cover and simmer 30 minutes. Add brisket and enough water just to cover. Return to simmer. Cover partially and cook until meat is fork tender, about 3 hours, skimming surface as necessary after first 15 minutes. *(Brisket can be prepared several hours ahead to this point. Set aside in cooking liquid at room temperature; reheat before continuing.)* Transfer to heated platter. Remove bay leaves from liquid and discard. Pour several spoonfuls of liquid over brisket and serve.

Tripe Stew with Calvados
(Tripes à la Mode de Caen)

6 servings

3 large carrots, peeled and sliced
2 large onions, sliced
   All purpose flour
2 pounds beef tripe, cleaned and
   cut into 2-inch pieces
1 calf's foot, split and cleaned
   Bouquet garni (3 parsley sprigs, 1
   fresh thyme sprig *or* ½ teaspoon
   dried, 1 bay leaf and 1 unpeeled
   garlic clove, tied together in a
   cheesecloth bag)

2 medium leeks, finely chopped
1 medium celery stalk, finely
   chopped
   Salt and freshly ground pepper
2 cups hard cider *or* dry white wine
2 tablespoons Calvados *or*
   applejack
½ cup all purpose flour
3½ tablespoons water

   Boiled potatoes

Preheat oven to 350°F. Dredge sliced carrots and onions in flour, shaking off excess. Transfer to deep baking dish with tight-fitting lid. Add tripe, calf's foot and bouquet garni. Sprinkle with leeks and celery. Season with salt and pepper. Add cider and Calvados. Mix ½ cup flour with water in small bowl to stiff paste. Cover baking dish and seal edge between cover and dish with flour paste. Place in oven just long enough to set seal, 5 to 10 minutes. Reduce oven temperature to 200°F and cook 10 hours.

   Discard bouquet garni and bones from calf's foot. Serve stew with potatoes.

2 ❦ Veal

It may seem hard to believe that veal and beef come from the same animal. Where beef is robust, red and resiliently firm in texture, everything about veal speaks of delicacy: its color paler, its texture much finer, its flavor subtle, almost sweet. Veal is, of course, the meat of calves at most four months old, and while its cuts are similar to those of beef, the distinctive qualities of veal call for different treatment in the kitchen.

The tenderest cuts of veal, from the ribs, loin and rump, are excellent for grilling, broiling or frying. But extra care must be taken to make sure that the delicate meat does not dry out. Thick veal chops or steaks, such as the Grilled Veal Chops Pizzaiola (page 30), or Veal Chops with Capers and Cream (page 36) stand up well to the direct heat of the grill or frying pan. Ground veal benefits from enrichments such as the breadcrumbs and half and half in Veal Cutlets Pojarsky (page 32). Thinner medallions, cutlets or scallops of veal are frequently coated before frying, and their texture and flavor are often complemented with rich, creamy sauces—as in Medallions of Veal in Three Mustard Sauce (page 36).

Larger rib, loin or rump cuts of veal are equally good for roasting or braising. To keep them moist in the oven, they are frequently stuffed, and examples in this chapter include a mixture of sun-dried tomatoes, oriental mushrooms, Herbes de Provence and garlic for Spit-roasted Stuffed Veal (page 43), and a creamy morel sauce for a Saddle of Veal (page 46). Enclosing the veal in a wrapper will also keep it moist as in Veal Chops en Papillote (page 46) and Phyllo-wrapped Veal Roll (page 48).

Like beef, the more muscular cuts of veal from the lower leg, shoulder and breast are best braised or poached. The recipes here are a further example of veal's compatibility with a wide range of ingredients, including Veal Ragout with Onions and Chestnuts (page 51), Italian Veal with Pesto and Orzo (page 52), and Veal and Sorrel Stew in Gougère Ring (page 56).

Whatever cut of veal you buy, look for meat that is bright and clear in color, with a firm but moist texture. The finest, youngest veal will have a creamy pink color indicating it was milk-fed. Older, grass-fed veal is a deeper rose color; though somewhat less tender and more pronounced in flavor, it will still exhibit the delicacy for which all good veal is prized.

🍃 Grilling

Grilled Veal Chops Pizzaiola

4 servings

4 8- to 9-ounce veal T-bone loin chops, about 1 inch thick
2 teaspoons olive oil
2 teaspoons dried oregano
  Salt and freshly ground pepper

4 teaspoons olive oil
1 medium onion, finely minced
1 16-ounce can Italian plum tomatoes with basil, drained and coarsely chopped (reserve juice)
2 large garlic cloves, flattened

1 teaspoon sugar
1 teaspoon dried basil
1 teaspoon dried oregano
8 anchovy fillets, pounded to smooth paste
4 teaspoons capers, rinsed and drained

  Minced Italian flat-leaf parsley (garnish)
4 lemon wedges (garnish)

Pat veal chops dry, then rub with 2 teaspoons oil, 2 teaspoons oregano and salt and pepper. Arrange in single layer in baking dish. Set aside at room temperature 2 hours.

Heat 4 teaspoons oil in heavy or nonstick large skillet over medium heat. Add onion and cook until wilted. Stir in chopped tomatoes, garlic, sugar, basil and 1 teaspoon oregano. Increase heat to medium high and cook until juices evaporate, about 5 minutes. Blend in reserved tomato juice with anchovy fillets. Cover partially and cook until thickened, about 10 minutes. Mix in capers and cook 5 minutes.

Grease broiler pan and position about 3 inches from heat source. Preheat pan and broiler. Transfer chops to heated pan. Cook, turning several times, until chops are juicy inside and charred and crusty outside, about 10 minutes total. Brush chops during last several minutes with any marinade remaining in dish. Transfer to individual plates. Nap evenly with sauce. Sprinkle with parsley. Garnish with lemon wedges.

🍃 Sautéing and Deep-frying

Veal Loin Chops with Cream and Chives

6 servings

6 lean veal loin chops, about 1½ inches thick (preferably first cut) and trimmed of excess fat, bones Frenched
  Salt and freshly ground pepper
1 cup all purpose flour

5 tablespoons clarified butter

1 cup dry white wine
1½ cups whipping cream
1 teaspoon Glace de Viande (meat glaze) (see recipe, page 11)
3 tablespoons snipped fresh chives
2 to 3 tablespoons unsalted butter
  Juice of ½ lemon

Preheat oven to lowest setting. Season chops on both sides with salt and pepper. Dip in flour, shaking off excess.

Melt butter in heavy 12-inch skillet over high heat until very hot. Add chops and sauté until richly browned, about 8 to 10 minutes per side, turning once and adjusting heat as necessary to prevent burning. Transfer to serving platter and keep warm in low oven.

Pour off any excess fat from skillet. Deglaze pan with wine. Boil over high heat until liquid is reduced to about ½ cup. Reduce heat to low, stir in cream and Glace de Viande and blend well. Add chives, butter and lemon juice and bring sauce just to simmer. Pour over chops and serve immediately.

Veal with Cucumbers and Morels

Serve with wild rice, braised celery and sautéed carrot, zucchini, cherry tomato halves, fiddlehead ferns or turnip.

6 servings

Champagne Sauce with Morels
1 cup dried morels (1½ ounces)
2 tablespoons (¼ stick) butter
1½ tablespoons minced shallot (about 1 large)
   Salt and freshly ground white pepper

2¼ cups dry white wine
1½ cups unsalted chicken stock
¾ cup chopped mushrooms *or* mushroom trimmings
6 medium shallots, minced

¼ cup plus 2 tablespoons dry Sherry
   Large pinch of dried thyme
4½ cups whipping cream

1 English cucumber, peeled
2 tablespoons (¼ stick) butter
1½ cups unsalted chicken stock

2 pounds boneless veal loin, cut into 12 even slices
   All purpose flour
3 tablespoons vegetable oil
2 tablespoons (¼ stick) butter

For Champagne sauce: Combine morels in medium bowl with just enough lukewarm water to cover. Let stand until water is clear, changing water about 5 times, about 1 hour total. Drain well. Pat dry. Trim off tough ends of stems. Cut each morel into halves or quarters, depending on size. Melt 2 tablespoons butter in large skillet over low heat. Add morels and 1½ tablespoons minced shallot and cook until morels are lightly glazed, stirring occasionally, about 10 minutes. Season with salt and white pepper. Reserve 24 uniform pieces of morel for garnish. Set remainder aside.

Combine wine, 1½ cups stock, mushrooms, remaining shallots, Sherry and thyme in large saucepan. Place over medium heat and cook until reduced to about 3 tablespoons. Add cream and cook until thickened, stirring occasionally. Strain through fine sieve set over bowl. Return sauce to large saucepan. Add morels. Place over medium-high heat and bring to simmer gently 10 to 15 minutes. Season to taste with salt and white pepper. Set sauce aside.

Cut cucumber crosswise into six 1½-inch-wide pieces. Cut each piece lengthwise into 4 slices. Melt 2 tablespoons butter in large skillet over medium-high heat. Add cucumber and sauté until just beginning to brown, about 4 minutes. Season with salt and white pepper. Add 1½ cups stock, reduce heat and poach gently until cucumber is lightly glazed. Set aside.

Season veal slices on both sides with salt and white pepper. Lightly dredge in flour, shaking off excess. Heat oil in heavy large skillet over medium heat. Add veal in batches (*do not crowd*) and cook until just beginning to color, about 1 minute. Add small amount of butter to skillet, adjusting heat if necessary to prevent butter from burning. When butter just begins to color light brown, turn veal with spatula. Continue cooking until veal is slightly firm when pressed with finger, about 3 minutes, watching carefully to prevent overcooking. Arrange veal on plates. Spoon sauce around veal. Garnish with reserved morels and poached cucumber slices. Serve immediately.

Veal Scaloppine with Mushroom Sauce

4 servings

Mushroom Sauce
- ¾ cup chicken stock
- 1 tablespoon all purpose flour
- 1 tablespoon butter
- 1 teaspoon finely chopped green onion (white part only)
- 1½ cups thinly sliced mushrooms
- ½ cup whipping cream
  Salt and freshly ground pepper
  Freshly grated nutmeg
  Pinch of ground red pepper

- 1 pound veal scallops *or*
  1 pound chicken breasts, skinned and boned
- 2 tablespoons all purpose flour
- 1 egg
- 2 tablespoons water
- 1½ cups breadcrumbs

- 3 to 5 tablespoons vegetable oil
- 1 to 2 tablespoons butter

For mushroom sauce: Combine stock and 1 tablespoon flour in small bowl and stir until flour is dissolved. Melt 1 tablespoon butter in medium skillet over medium-high heat. Add onion and sauté until tender, about 1 minute. Reduce heat to medium. Add mushrooms and cook about 2 to 3 minutes. Stir in stock. Increase heat to medium high and cook until slightly thickened, stirring occasionally, about 10 minutes. Blend in cream. Season to taste with salt and pepper, nutmeg and red pepper. Set aside and keep warm.

Pound meat between 2 sheets of waxed paper until very thin. Season 2 tablespoons flour with salt and pepper in pie plate. Beat egg with water in shallow dish. Dredge meat in flour, dip into egg mixture and then roll in breadcrumbs. Lightly pound slices with flat of knife so breadcrumbs adhere to meat.

Heat 3 tablespoons oil with 1 tablespoon butter in large skillet over medium-high heat. Add meat in batches and sauté until browned, turning once, about 3 to 5 minutes, adding more oil and butter as necessary. Transfer to platter and spoon sauce over top.

Veal Cutlets Pojarsky

8 servings

- 1 cup fresh breadcrumbs
- ½ cup half and half

- 1 pound veal stew meat
- 1 pound chicken breasts, skinned and boned

- 1 teaspoon salt
- ½ teaspoon freshly ground pepper
- 16 tablespoons (2 sticks) butter, softened

- 2 tablespoons (¼ stick) butter

- ½ pound mushrooms, sliced
- ½ teaspoon salt
- ¼ teaspoon freshly ground pepper
  Juice of ½ lemon

- 1 cup fine breadcrumbs

- 2 tablespoons (¼ stick) butter
- ¼ cup dry white wine
- 1 teaspoon arrowroot dissolved in 1 teaspoon water
- 1 lemon, sliced (garnish)

Combine breadcrumbs and half and half in small bowl and set aside to soak.

Meanwhile, grind veal and chicken through fine blade of grinder. Repeat. Transfer ground meat mixture to large bowl.

Squeeze excess moisture from breadcrumbs through tea cloth. Add breadcrumbs, 1 teaspoon salt and ½ teaspoon pepper to meat mixture. Stir in butter 1 tablespoon at a time, blending well. Cover and refrigerate 1 hour.

Melt 2 tablespoons butter in medium skillet over medium heat. Add mushrooms and sprinkle with ½ teaspoon salt, ¼ teaspoon pepper and lemon juice. Cover with buttered waxed paper and top skillet with lid. Steam mushrooms 4 to 5 minutes, shaking pan frequently to prevent sticking. Remove from heat. Strain liquid into small bowl and transfer mushrooms to another bowl. Set aside.

Roll meat mixture into 12-inch cylinder. Chill 15 minutes. Cut cylinder into 1¼-inch slices. Flatten and shape into choplike portions. Roll in breadcrumbs, coating completely. *(Cutlets can be prepared ahead to this point and refrigerated.)*

Melt remaining butter in large skillet over medium-high heat. Add cutlets and sauté 5 to 7 minutes per side. Set aside and keep warm. Deglaze pan with wine, scraping up any browned bits clinging to bottom. Add reserved mushroom liquid and dissolved arrowroot. Stir until sauce is thickened. Strain; return to skillet. Add mushrooms, stirring to blend. Taste and adjust seasoning. To serve, spoon sauce onto heated platter. Arrange cutlets over sauce and garnish with lemon slices.

Veal Chops with Mushroom Sauce

4 servings

½ cup all purpose flour
½ teaspoon salt
¼ teaspoon freshly ground pepper
4 veal shoulder chops, trimmed
4 tablespoons (½ stick) butter
1 small onion, chopped

½ pound mushrooms, sliced
½ cup dry white wine
2 cups beef stock

Freshly cooked noodles

Combine flour, salt and pepper in paper bag. Dredge chops in flour one at a time, shaking off excess. Melt 2½ tablespoons butter in heavy skillet over low heat. Add onion. Cover and cook, stirring occasionally, until onion is translucent, about 10 minutes. Add mushrooms, increase heat to medium high and cook uncovered, stirring frequently, until mushrooms are tender and juices have evaporated, about 5 minutes. Blend in wine and bring to boil. Let boil until reduced by half. Stir in beef stock. Remove from heat.

Melt remaining 1½ tablespoons butter in another heavy skillet over medium heat. Add veal and cook, turning frequently, until almost tender, about 15 minutes. Pour mushroom sauce over veal. Reduce heat and simmer until sauce is thickened, about 5 minutes. Arrange over noodles and serve immediately.

Herbed Veal with Lemon

4 servings

8 veal scallops (about 1⅓ ounces each)
Salt and freshly ground pepper
½ cup all purpose flour
¼ cup (½ stick) butter
1 tablespoon vegetable oil
2 tablespoons dry white wine
½ cup chicken stock

2 tablespoons fresh lemon juice
1 tablespoon finely chopped green onion
1 tablespoon minced fresh parsley
2 small sprigs fresh rosemary *or* ½ teaspoon dried
Freshly cooked rice *or* pasta
Lemon wedges (garnish)

Season veal with salt and pepper. Dredge veal in flour to coat well, shaking off excess. Melt butter with oil in heavy skillet over medium-high heat until hot but not smoking. Add veal and brown quickly on both sides, turning frequently. Transfer veal to heated platter. Pour wine into skillet and stir, scraping up any browned bits. Blend in stock, lemon juice, onion, parsley and rosemary. Reduce heat, cover and simmer gently, stirring frequently, 3 to 5 minutes. Return veal to skillet. Cover and simmer gently until tender, about 1 to 2 minutes. Spoon veal over rice or pasta. Serve immediately with lemon.

Veal Monterey

6 to 8 servings

8 thin slices avocado
16 veal scallops (about 2 pounds total), pounded thin
8 thin slices tomato, drained on paper towels
8 slices Monterey Jack cheese
8 tablespoons freshly grated Parmesan cheese

Salt and freshly ground pepper
8 ounces cooked tiny shrimp

All purpose flour
2 eggs, beaten
2 cups breadcrumbs

2 to 4 tablespoons clarified butter
Lemon wedges (garnish)

Arrange 1 avocado slice over veal scallop. Top with 1 tomato slice and 1 slice Monterey Jack cheese. Sprinkle with 1 tablespoon Parmesan. Season with salt and pepper to taste. Top with 1 ounce shrimp. Cover with another veal scallop. Pinch edges of veal together tightly to form packet. Transfer to plate. Repeat with remaining veal, avocado, tomato, cheese and shrimp. Refrigerate until firm, about 1 to 1½ hours.

Dust veal with flour, shaking off excess. Dip into beaten egg and then coat with breadcrumbs.

Heat butter in large skillet over medium-high heat. Add veal in batches (*do not crowd*) and sauté until lightly browned, about 3 to 5 minutes per side. Transfer veal to platter. Garnish with lemon.

Stuffed Veal Medallions with Taleggio Sauce

Sautéed red peppers and zucchini are a lovely accompaniment.

6 servings

1 cup whipping cream
2 tablespoons cornstarch
4 ounces Taleggio cheese, grated *or* sliced
Salt and freshly ground pepper

6 1-inch-thick veal medallions from tenderloin (about 18 ounces total)
3 ounces prosciutto, finely chopped
2 large garlic cloves, mashed to puree
2 tablespoons minced fresh Italian flat-leaf parsley
All purpose flour

1 egg
1 tablespoon water
1 tablespoon vegetable oil
½ cup fresh breadcrumbs
½ cup toasted hazelnuts, skinned and finely chopped (toast 10 minutes at 350°F)

6 tablespoons (¾ stick) butter
Parsley sprigs (garnish)

Gradually blend cream into cornstarch in heavy small saucepan. Bring to boil over low heat, stirring constantly. Remove from heat. Add cheese and stir until smooth. Season to taste with salt and pepper. Set sauce aside at room temperature until ready to use.

Make horizontal slit in side of each veal medallion, cutting ⅔ way through to form pocket. Combine prosciutto, garlic and parsley. Fill each pocket with mixture. Press to close.

Season flour with salt and pepper. Blend egg, water, oil and salt and pepper in small bowl. Mix breadcrumbs and hazelnuts. Flour each medallion, shaking off excess. Brush each evenly with egg mixture, then coat with crumbs.

Melt butter in heavy large skillet over medium-high heat. Add veal and brown quickly on each side. Sprinkle with salt and pepper. Top with sauce. Cover and cook until cheese is melted and meat is done, about 7 minutes. Transfer veal to platter. Garnish with parsley sprigs and serve.

Veal Bontemps

This dish is served in individual casseroles. With its flavorful sauce, Veal Bontemps is also excellent over rice.

8 servings

6 tablespoons (¾ stick) butter
⅔ cup all purpose flour
1½ cups chicken stock
1½ cups beef stock
1½ cups apple juice
2 medium Winesap apples, peeled, cored and finely chopped
¼ cup Dijon mustard

½ cup (1 stick) butter
2 pounds veal leg, trimmed and cut julienne
8 medium mushrooms, trimmed and sliced
Salt and freshly ground pepper

Melt 6 tablespoons butter in large saucepan over medium-low heat. Add flour and stir until mixture begins to color, about 4 minutes. Whisk in stocks and apple juice. Increase heat to medium and simmer 5 minutes, stirring frequently. Blend in chopped apples and mustard and cook 1 minute. Remove sauce from heat.

Melt ½ cup butter in heavy large skillet over medium-high heat. Add veal and mushrooms, season with salt and pepper and sauté until veal is nearly cooked through, about 3 to 4 minutes. Stir in sauce and simmer until mushrooms are tender, about 3 to 4 minutes. Serve immediately.

Egyptian Veal Cutlets

8 servings

2⅔ pounds veal scallops
2 cups finely ground unsalted cracker crumbs
½ teaspoon cinnamon
½ teaspoon freshly ground white pepper

Dash of freshly grated nutmeg
Salt
3 eggs, beaten to blend
1 cup (2 sticks) butter

Pound scallops until very thin. Combine cracker crumbs, cinnamon, pepper, nutmeg and salt in shallow bowl and mix well. Dip each scallop first in eggs, then in crumb mixture, coating well. Melt butter in large skillet over medium-high heat. Add veal (in batches if necessary; *do not crowd*) and sauté just until done, about 2 minutes on each side. Serve immediately.

Veal la Louisiane

A popular dish from the Lodge Alley Inn in Charleston, South Carolina.

4 servings

4 2½-ounce slices boneless veal
Salt and freshly ground white pepper
All purpose flour
2 tablespoons vegetable oil
½ pound mushrooms, sliced
2 cups whipping cream

¼ cup Madeira
¼ cup (½ stick) butter, cut into 12 pieces
4 ounces cooked crabmeat
8 cooked jumbo shrimp, shelled and deveined
4 poached crayfish (optional)

Pound veal to thickness of ¼ inch. Season with salt and pepper. Dredge lightly in flour, shaking off excess. Heat oil in large skillet over medium heat. Add veal and brown 45 seconds on each side. Transfer veal to platter and keep warm. Add mushrooms to skillet and sauté 5 minutes. Add cream and Madeira and reduce until thickened, about 15 minutes. Season with salt and pepper. Stir in butter 1 piece at a time, incorporating each piece completely before adding next. Add crabmeat and shrimp and heat through, about 1 minute. Pour over veal. Top each slice with 1 poached crayfish if desired. Serve immediately.

Medallions of Veal in Three-Mustard Sauce
(Medaillon de Veau aux Trois Moutardes)

A popular entrée at L'Orangerie in Los Angeles.

6 servings

12 2- to 3-ounce veal medallions, pounded to about ¼ inch
   Salt and freshly ground pepper
 3 tablespoons butter
 6 medium shallots, minced
1½ cups dry white wine
 1 cup veal stock

 3 cups whipping cream, or more
⅓ cup tarragon mustard
⅓ cup Dijon mustard
⅓ cup coarse-ground French mustard (moutarde de Meaux)
   Steamed and pureed fresh vegetables (garnish)

Season veal with salt and pepper to taste. Heat 1 tablespoon butter in large skillet over medium-high heat. Add veal in 2 batches and sauté until just cooked, about 2 minutes on each side, adding about 1 more tablespoon butter to skillet after first batch. Transfer veal to heated platter and keep warm. Return skillet to medium-high heat. Add shallots and sauté until softened, about 1 minute. Blend in wine and stock, increase heat to high and cook until reduced to syrupy consistency. Stir in 3 cups cream and reduce to saucelike consistency. Reduce heat to medium low. Add mustards and blend well; do not return to boil or sauce will be grainy. If sauce seems too thick, thin with small amount of cream. Swirl in remaining 1 tablespoon butter, blending until smooth. Adjust seasoning. Spoon sauce over veal. Garnish with vegetables and serve.

Veal Chops with Capers and Cream

Chicken breasts can be substituted for veal.

6 servings

6 veal loin chops, about ¾ inch thick
2 tablespoons (¼ stick) butter
2 tablespoons olive oil
  Salt and freshly ground pepper

2 tablespoons minced shallot
½ cup beef stock

¼ cup dry vermouth
1 tablespoon fresh lemon juice, or to taste
½ cup whipping cream
2 tablespoons capers, rinsed and drained
2 tablespoons minced fresh parsley

Preheat oven to 200°F. Pat veal dry with paper towels. Melt butter with oil in heavy large skillet over medium heat. Add veal (in batches if necessary; *do not crowd*) and brown on one side, about 7 minutes. Turn chops over. Season with salt and pepper. Continue cooking until just springy to touch and pink in center, about 7 minutes. Transfer to heated platter. Cover and place in oven, leaving door ajar.

Pour off all but 2 tablespoons fat in skillet. Add shallot and stir 2 minutes. Add stock, vermouth and lemon juice and boil until reduced by half, scraping up any brown bits. Stir in cream and capers. Simmer until thickened to saucelike consistency. Adjust seasoning. Pour sauce over veal. Sprinkle with parsley and serve.

Sautéed Sweetbreads and Mushrooms
(Poêlée de Cèpes et Ris de Veau)

4 servings

1 pound veal sweetbreads

¼ cup walnut oil
1 tablespoon white wine vinegar
½ teaspoon Dijon mustard
  Salt and freshly ground pepper

6 tablespoons (¾ stick) butter
¾ pound cèpes, soaked 1 hour in
  cold water and drained, *or* ¾
  pound mushrooms

Pinch *each* of finely chopped
  shallot, chervil, chives and parsley

1 large bunch fresh spinach,
  washed and stemmed (garnish)

Soak sweetbreads in large bowl of water for several hours, changing water frequently until clear. Drain sweetbreads well; remove connective tissue. Transfer sweetbreads to medium saucepan and cover with cold water. Bring to boil slowly over medium heat. Reduce heat to low and simmer 5 minutes. Drain sweetbreads well; rinse under cold water. Place between two plates and weight with heavy object to flatten. Cover and refrigerate several hours. Cut sweetbreads into ¼-inch slices and set aside.

Combine walnut oil, vinegar, mustard and salt and pepper in jar with tight-fitting lid and shake well.

Melt 2 tablespoons butter in medium skillet over medium-high heat. Add cèpes and sauté until liquid is released. Drain liquid from skillet. Add shallot, chervil, chives and parsley to skillet. Season to taste with salt and pepper and sauté 2 to 3 minutes. Add 3 to 4 tablespoons dressing and toss cèpes carefully. Keep cèpes warm.

Melt 2 tablespoons butter in large skillet over high heat. Add sweetbreads and sauté on both sides until browned, about 3 to 4 minutes. Set aside.

Melt remaining 2 tablespoons butter in medium skillet over medium-high heat. Add spinach and cook just until wilted. Sprinkle with salt and pepper. Divide sweetbreads among 4 plates. Top with cèpes. Garnish with spinach.

Veal and Beef Dijonnaise

6 servings

2 tablespoons butter *or* vegetable
  oil
5 small shallots, chopped
10 ounces veal, trimmed and cut into
  strips
10 ounces beef fillet, trimmed and
  cut into strips
5 ounces mushrooms, sliced (about
  6 large)

½ cup dry white wine
½ cup brandy
3 cups whipping cream
1½ cups demi-glace
2 teaspoons Glace de Viande (meat
  glaze) (see recipe, page 11)
½ teaspoon freshly ground white
  pepper
3½ tablespoons Dijon mustard

Melt butter in heavy large skillet over medium-low heat. Add shallots and cook until tender, about 2 minutes. Increase heat to medium high, add veal, beef and mushrooms and sauté 2 minutes. Remove mixture from skillet, set aside and keep warm. Reduce heat to medium. Add wine and brandy to skillet and ignite, shaking skillet gently until flame subsides. Stir in cream, demi-glace, Glace de Viande and pepper. Increase heat to medium high and cook until thickened to desired consistency. Remove from heat and blend in mustard. Stir in meat and mushrooms and serve.

🍎 Classic Brown Sauce and Variations

The classic brown sauce is one of the *sauces mères* (mother sauces) of French cuisine, so called because many other important sauces are derived from it. Like the white sauces, béchamel and velouté, brown sauce consists of a liquid thickened with a cooked mixture of butter and flour called a roux. The difference is that for a brown sauce the roux is cooked much longer; it must be stirred over low heat until it acquires a nut-brown cast that intensifies the color and flavor of the sauce. This lengthier cooking diminishes the thickening power of the starch, a factor that should be taken into consideration before you start cooking. To make a brown sauce of medium thickness, allow 2 tablespoons of both butter and flour for each cup of liquid.

Another major difference between the white and brown sauce families is the liquid on which they are based. Instead of milk, chicken, veal or fish stock, brown sauce takes much of its flavor and character from a substantial beef stock that has been flavored with browned beef bones or veal bones.

Some of the most important sauces in French cuisine—Madère, Bordelaise, Poivrade—are among the spin-offs of the Classic Brown Sauce. And, as the recipes for these and other variations indicate, the basic structure of these sauces is identical to that of the mother sauce; only the flavorings change. A rich-tasting brown sauce is a perfect match for aged beef, and its variations include ideal partners for veal, lamb and pork.

A brown sauce that is the color of mahogany, with rich, concentrated flavor and a silken sheen, is not difficult to make, but it does take time. The sauce must simmer for 3 to 4 hours in order to attain the desired consistency and intensity of flavor. One taste of a carefully simmered and perfectly seasoned brown sauce and you will understand why many chefs consider a Sauce Madère or a Sauce Bordelaise, or any of their cousins, among the triumphs of the good cook's repertoire.

Classic Brown Sauce
_____

Makes 1 quart

- 2 tablespoons (¼ stick) unsalted butter
- 1 medium onion, thinly sliced
- 1 medium carrot, diced
- 1 celery stalk, including leaves, thinly sliced
- 1 ounce prosciutto *or* other ham, diced

- ½ cup (1 stick) unsalted butter
- ½ cup all purpose flour
- 2 quarts degreased rich unsalted beef stock, at boiling point
- 10 parsley sprigs (with stems)
- 6 sprigs fresh thyme *or* 2 teaspoons dried

- 2 bay leaves
- 1 tablespoon tomato paste *or* 2 large tomatoes, coarsely chopped
- 1 large shallot, minced
- 1 large garlic clove, minced
  Mushroom trimmings (optional)
  Chicken, beef, veal *or* ham trimmings and bones (optional)
- 2 tablespoons Cognac
  Salt and freshly ground pepper

Melt 2 tablespoons butter in heavy 4-quart saucepan over low heat. Add onion, carrot, celery and prosciutto. Cover and cook 15 minutes, stirring occasionally. Transfer to bowl.

Melt ½ cup butter in same saucepan over low heat. Add flour and stir until roux is the color of coffee with cream, about 10 minutes. Whisk in boiling stock. Increase heat and stir until sauce returns to boil. Add reserved onion mixture to saucepan with parsley, thyme, bay leaves, tomato paste, shallot, garlic and trimmings and bones. Reduce heat and simmer, skimming off foam that rises to surface, until sauce has thickened and is reduced to 4 cups, about 3 hours, stirring occasionally toward end of cooking time to prevent sticking. Strain sauce through chinois or sieve lined with 3 layers of dampened cheesecloth, *but do not press down on ingredients or sauce will be cloudy.* Remove any fat from surface of sauce by blotting with strips of paper towel. Just before serving, stir in Cognac and season with salt and pepper.

Enrichments for Classic Brown Sauce

Enhance the Classic Brown Sauce with any or all of the following enrichments:

Butter: For a shiny gloss, whisk 2 tablespoons (¼ stick) well-chilled butter into sauce just before serving. Do not reheat or sauce will separate.

Caramel: Caramel naturally deepens the color of a sauce without noticeably affecting its flavor. To prepare caramel, place 2 teaspoons sugar in heavy small saucepan (do not use tin-lined copper) and melt over low heat. Let cook until lightly golden in color. Turn off heat, stand away from pan and pour in ladleful of sauce. Stir over low heat until well blended. Strain into remaining sauce and mix thoroughly.

Glace de Viande: To heighten flavor, stir in a tablespoon of glace de viande (meat glaze) when reheating sauce.

Deglazing Juices: After meat is cooked, discard any fat in pan. Pour in 1 cup white or red wine or Madeira and boil until reduced to ¼ cup, scraping up any browned bits clinging to bottom of pan. Strain into sauce and blend well.

Variations on Classic Brown Sauce

Sauce Madère: Combine ⅓ cup Madeira, Sherry or Port with 1 cup brown sauce in heavy saucepan and simmer 20 minutes, stirring occasionally. Serve with beef.

Sauce Périgueux: With truffles, a Sauce Madère becomes the exquisite Sauce Périgueux. Splendid with beef, it is generally reserved for special occasions. Slice 1 fresh or canned truffle and marinate in ½ cup Madeira for at least 24 hours. Melt 2 tablespoons (¼ stick) butter in small saucepan over medium heat. Add 1 minced small shallot and stir until translucent. Add truffle and marinade. Simmer gently 10 minutes. Remove truffle using slotted spoon. Set aside. Boil marinade until reduced to ¼ cup. Add truffle and 1 cup brown sauce and simmer 5 minutes.

Sauce Bordelaise: Soak 4 inches beef marrow in ice water overnight. Combine ¾ cup dry red wine, 1 minced medium shallot and 1 sprig fresh thyme (or 1 teaspoon dried thyme) in small saucepan and boil until reduced to 2 tablespoons. Strain into another saucepan. Add 1 cup brown sauce and simmer 5 minutes, stirring occasionally. Drain marrow and slice into pieces ¼ inch thick. Transfer to small saucepan. Cover with cold salted water and heat just until water simmers. Drain again. Reserve a slice to garnish each serving; stir remainder into sauce. A traditional accompaniment for beef.

(continued on next page)

(continued from page 39)

Sauce Marchand de Vin: Melt 2 tablespoons (¼ stick) butter in heavy small saucepan over medium-high heat. Add 1 minced large shallot and 1½ cups sliced mushrooms and sauté until mushroom juices have evaporated, about 5 minutes. Stir in ¾ cup dry red wine. Increase heat and boil until mixture is reduced to ¼ cup. Stir in 1 cup brown sauce and 1 teaspoon fresh lemon juice. Simmer 5 minutes, stirring occasionally. The only brown sauce variation to be created in America, this is usually spooned over beef.

Sauce Poivrade: Melt 1 tablespoon butter in heavy small saucepan over low heat. Add ¼ cup thinly sliced onion and ¼ cup thinly sliced carrot. Cover and cook until translucent, stirring occasionally, about 10 minutes. Stir in 1 bay leaf, 1 sprig fresh thyme (or 1 teaspoon dried thyme), ¾ cup dry red wine and 2 tablespoons red wine vinegar. Increase heat and boil until reduced to ¼ cup. Strain into another saucepan. Add 1 cup brown sauce. Stir in ½ teaspoon coarsely crushed black peppercorns. Simmer 5 minutes, stirring occasionally. A traditional sauce for lamb. By adding 1 tablespoon currant jelly and 2 tablespoons whipping cream this variation becomes a *Grand Veneur.*

Quick Brown Sauces

Jus Lié: Boil 2 cups rich beef stock until reduced to 1 cup. Dissolve 2 teaspoons cornstarch in 1 tablespoon of the sauce. Stir into remaining sauce. Cook over medium heat until thickened. Or mix 2 tablespoons all purpose flour and 2 tablespoons (¼ stick) softened butter for a beurre manié. Whisk into boiling sauce. Remove from heat as soon as beurre manié is fully incorporated into sauce.

Deglazing Sauce: After meat has cooked, pour out any fat from skillet or roasting pan. Add 2 cups rich stock and boil until reduced to 1 cup. Thicken with cornstarch or beurre manié as described above. Or place over low heat and swirl in 4 tablespoons (½ stick) butter 1 tablespoon at a time.

Great Hints

- Rendered beef, veal or pork fat can be substituted for butter in recipe for Classic Brown Sauce.
- To hasten browning of roux, precook flour in a 350°F oven for 20 minutes, stirring occasionally.
- For a fat-free brown sauce, place ½ cup oven-browned flour in a saucepan and whisk in enough brown stock to make a paste. Gradually whisk in remaining stock (there should be a total of 2 cups stock) and bring to a boil. Sieve if necessary. Add raw onion, carrot, celery, shallot, garlic and other seasonings and proceed as for Classic Brown Sauce.
- A brown sauce should be thick enough to cling to food without overwhelming it. If it is too thick, thin with cream or stock. If it is too thin, reduce over high heat or thicken with a beurre manié.
- Add acidic ingredients such as vinegar, lemon or lime juice after the sauce has reduced. If added earlier, sauce won't thicken.
- To keep sauce warm, place in a double boiler. Do not cover or steam will thin sauce too much.

Italian Sausage Rolled in Veal

6 servings

3 hot Italian sausages, cut in half crosswise

6 boneless veal cutlets

2 tablespoons freshly grated Parmesan cheese

2 tablespoons finely chopped fresh parsley

1 teaspoon fennel seed, crushed
1 garlic clove, crushed
   All purpose flour

2 cups vegetable oil
6 ounces mushrooms, sliced

2 tablespoons (¼ stick) butter
1 cup dry Sherry

Prick sausages all over with point of sharp knife. Transfer sausages to large skillet. Place over medium heat and fry until browned and cooked through, about 30 minutes. Drain on paper towels.

Pound cutlets until large enough to enclose sausage completely without overlap.

Combine cheese, parsley, fennel seed and garlic in small bowl and mix well. Divide among cutlets, spreading evenly. Place 1 sausage along 1 edge of cutlet. Roll up and tie securely with string. Roll in flour, shaking off excess. Repeat with remaining sausages and cutlets.

Heat oil in deep large skillet or deep fryer until hot (about 375°F). Add veal rolls and fry until golden brown. Drain on paper towels. Set aside and keep warm. Add mushrooms to hot oil and fry until browned, about 1 to 2 minutes. Remove with slotted spoon and drain well.

Melt butter in large skillet over medium-high heat. Add Sherry and cook until thickened, about 5 to 10 minutes. Stir in mushrooms. Arrange veal rolls on platter and cover with sauce. Serve immediately.

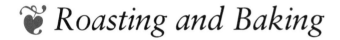 Roasting and Baking

Rolled Boneless Veal Loin Stuffed with Truffles

Pork can be used instead of veal. Roast at 500°F until golden brown, about 15 to 20 minutes, then reduce heat to 325°F and continue roasting, covered, about 2 hours.

8 to 10 servings

1 5-pound boneless veal loin, trimmed of all fat
1 garlic clove, mashed
1 .9-ounce can truffles, thickly sliced (reserve liquid from can) *or* ¼ cup Duxelles (see following recipes)
¼ cup olive oil

   Salt and freshly ground pepper

¼ cup wine vinegar
1 cup chicken stock
   Herbed Brandy Sauce (see following recipes)

Preheat oven to 500°F. Make lengthwise pocket in meat. Rub pocket with garlic. Stuff with truffle slices or Duxelles. Roll meat lengthwise and tie at 1-inch intervals with string. Rub with oil and sprinkle with salt and pepper.

Set on rack in shallow pan and roast until golden, about 15 to 20 minutes. Reduce oven temperature to 375°F. Sprinkle meat with vinegar and pour chicken stock and liquid from truffles into pan. Cover and continue roasting until done, about 1½ hours. Transfer to heated platter and serve with sauce.

Duxelles

Makes about 2 cups

½ cup (1 stick) unsalted butter
3 tablespoons olive oil
2 pounds mushrooms, minced
½ cup minced shallot *or* green onion (white part only)
Bouquet garni (1 bay leaf, ½ teaspoon dried thyme and a few parsley sprigs, tied together in a cheesecloth bag)

½ cup Madeira *or* ¼ cup brown stock
Salt and freshly ground pepper

Heat butter and olive oil in 10- or 12-inch skillet over low heat. Add mushrooms and shallot and stir well. Add bouquet garni and cook until most of moisture has evaporated, about 40 to 45 minutes. (Mushrooms will turn dark and begin to separate into pieces.)

Add Madeira and continue cooking until all liquid has evaporated and mushrooms are almost black, about 2 hours. Remove bouquet garni. Taste and season with salt and pepper.

Herbed Brandy Sauce

½ cup Cognac
2 tablespoons fresh *or* dried rosemary leaves
¼ cup (½ stick) unsalted butter

4 cups whipping cream
Pan juices from veal roast
1 teaspoon salt
¼ teaspoon freshly ground pepper

Combine Cognac and rosemary in small pan and let stand 15 minutes.

Heat butter in heavy 4-quart saucepan over medium-high heat until bubbling. Heat ⅓ of Cognac. Ignite and add to butter. Repeat 2 more times (keep lid handy to cover pan if flame gets too high).

Gradually add cream and stir constantly with wooden spoon until sauce has reduced by ⅔ and thickened, about 15 to 20 minutes. *(Sauce can be made several days ahead to this point.)*

Skim as much fat as possible from pan juices. If necessary, boil juices until no more than ⅓ cup remains. Stir in cream mixture and whisk to combine thoroughly. Season with salt and pepper. Transfer to heated sauceboat.

Spit-roasted Stuffed Veal with Thyme Butter

The boneless veal roast is filled with sun-dried tomatoes, oriental mushrooms, Herbes de Provence and garlic.

10 servings

Stuffing
1 ounce shiitake *or* other dried black mushrooms (about 1 cup)
2 tablespoons (¼ stick) unsalted butter
2 tablespoons chopped shallot
1 small garlic clove, minced
¾ cup dried French breadcrumbs
½ cup (1 stick) unsalted butter, melted
½ cup sun-dried tomatoes packed in olive oil, drained and sliced (reserve oil)
2 teaspoons Herbes de Provence
Salt and freshly ground pepper

1 8-pound veal sirloin *or* rump roast, boned
1 tablespoon Dijon mustard
2 teaspoons Herbes de Provence
¼ teaspoon salt
Freshly ground pepper

Thyme Butter
1 cup (2 sticks) butter, room temperature
1 tablespoon fresh lemon juice
1 teaspoon minced fresh thyme *or* ¼ teaspoon dried
1 teaspoon chopped fresh parsley

Chopped fresh parsley (garnish)

For stuffing: Cover dried mushrooms with warm water in small bowl. Let stand until softened, about 30 minutes. Drain well and pat dry. Slice mushrooms into ½-inch-wide strips, discarding hard cores.

Melt 2 tablespoons butter in large skillet over medium heat. Add shallot, garlic and mushrooms and stir until shallot is limp, about 2 minutes. Transfer mixture to large bowl. Add breadcrumbs, melted butter, tomatoes and 2 teaspoons Herbes de Provence with salt and pepper to taste.

Open boned veal on work surface. Season lightly with salt and pepper. Spoon stuffing evenly down center. Roll veal up around stuffing and tie firmly at 1½-inch intervals; *do not tie too tightly or stuffing will come out of ends*. Mix mustard, remaining Herbes de Provence and salt and pepper with reserved tomato oil in small bowl. Rub mixture over entire surface of veal. Skewer veal and arrange on rotisserie. (Veal can also be roasted in 350°F oven.) Roast until veal is slightly pink, juices run clear when pricked with fork and meat thermometer inserted in thickest part of meat registers 160°F, about 1½ hours.

For thyme butter: Mix butter, lemon juice, thyme and 1 teaspoon parsley in small bowl. Roll into cylinder, refrigerate and cut into pats, or pack into individual ramekins. Serve butter at room temperature.

Let veal stand 20 minutes before carving. Arrange on serving platter. Top with parsley. Serve with thyme butter.

🍒 Brown Stock

Whenever a sauce or soup has particularly good flavor, its quality may well be credited to the stock used to make it. One of the most useful is brown stock, a savory liquid made from the slow simmering of browned veal or beef, vegetables, seasonings and water. It provides the flavor base for innumerable soups, sauces, stews and vegetable dishes. When cooked down until most of the liquid has evaporated, brown sauce becomes Glace de Viande (meat glaze), a potent beef concentrate (1 teaspoon of glace de viande combined with 1 quart water makes 1 quart of beef stock).

It is important to make brown stock from only the best ingredients available. Use the tougher, more flavorful cuts of meat. Bones and vegetables must be fresh. Even the water should be pure and free from off flavors. The stock may leave its signature on a dozen meals—it should be the very best you can make.

Brown Stock

Makes 5 to 6 cups

3 tablespoons vegetable oil
3 pounds veal *or* beef shank *or* other veal *or* beef cut with bones
3 pounds bottom round, chuck, sirloin *or* other lean stewing beef

3 medium carrots, sliced
3 celery stalks, including leaves, cut into 2-inch pieces
1 large onion, quartered

1 large onion, peeled, studded with 4 whole cloves
4 garlic cloves, unpeeled and lightly crushed
2 bay leaves
1 teaspoon black peppercorns
3 parsley sprigs
½ teaspoon dried thyme
4 to 5 quarts water (preferably purified drinking water)

Preheat oven to 375°F. Pour oil into large, shallow roasting pan. Place bones and meat in pan, turning to coat with oil. Roast uncovered 30 minutes.

Add remaining ingredients except water. Roast an additional 30 minutes. Transfer meat and vegetables to a 12- to 16-quart stockpot. Add 1 quart water to roasting pan. Bring to boil over high heat, scraping brown bits from bottom and sides of pan. Pour contents of roasting pan into stockpot and add enough water to cover meat and bones, about 3 to 4 quarts. Place uncovered over medium heat and bring slowly to a boil, about 30 minutes. (Slow heating helps extract juices from meat, making a more flavorful stock. If water is brought too rapidly to a boil, nutrients and flavor will be sealed in rather than released into the stock.) Reduce heat and simmer uncovered 8 hours. Skim off film as it rises to the surface.

Remove meat and vegetables with slotted spoon. Strain stock through fine sieve. Refrigerate several hours or overnight. When stock is cold, remove solidified fat from surface.

Variations on Brown Stock

Glace de Viande (meat glaze): Glace de viande will keep in the refrigerator for several months in a tightly closed jar. If molding should occur, wash away with hot water—glace de viande is still good. It can also be frozen: place teaspoonfuls into small plastic bags and defrost as needed.

Place 4 cups brown stock in a 2-quart saucepan. Cook uncovered over medium heat 1 to 1½ hours. As it reduces, transfer it to successively smaller saucepans; this lessens the chance of burning glaze. As stock is reduced, it will become syrupy and coat the back of a metal spoon. When allowed to stand, it will solidify.

Clarified Brown Stock

Makes about 4 cups

4 cups fat-free stock, chilled
1 egg white, lightly beaten

1 eggshell, crushed

Combine all ingredients in 2-quart saucepan. Stir over low heat just until stock boils. Cook uncovered over very low heat 20 minutes. Let stand 15 minutes. Strain through a colander lined with several layers of dampened cheesecloth.

Consommé Double: Follow directions for clarified stock, adding 1 pound lean ground beef. Cook 1 hour. Chill completely, then degrease.

Great Hints

- Add a tablespoon of cold water to simmering stock; this causes more film to rise to the surface and decreases the number of times you will need to skim.
- Do not use pork, lamb or starchy vegetables such as potatoes to make brown stock.
- Salt is not used in the preparation of brown stock because salt does not cook away along with the liquid. Plan on salting to taste when using stock in other dishes.
- Stock will keep in refrigerator a minimum of 3 days. After 3 days, either bring to a boil and rechill or freeze in batches. An empty milk carton is a good freezer container.

Saddle of Veal with Morel Sauce

4 servings

Veal
1 22-ounce whole saddle of veal, trimmed of silver skin
   Salt and freshly ground white pepper
   All purpose flour
¼ cup (½ stick) clarified butter

Morel Sauce
16 dried morels
 1 cup hot water

1 tablespoon butter
1 heaping tablespoon finely chopped shallot
¼ cup Calvados *or* applejack
1 cup whipping cream
½ cup veal demi-glace
   Salt and freshly ground white pepper

For veal: Preheat oven to 450°F. Sprinkle veal with salt and white pepper, then coat with flour. Melt ¼ cup butter in large ovenproof skillet over medium-high heat. Add veal and sear well on all sides, about 1 to 2 minutes. Transfer to oven and roast until meat thermometer inserted in center registers 140°F to 150°F, about 6 to 10 minutes. Set aside and keep warm.

For morel sauce: Rinse morels thoroughly. Transfer to bowl and cover with 1 cup hot water. Let stand 10 minutes.

Melt butter in medium saucepan over medium-high heat. Add shallot and sauté until transparent. Warm Calvados in small saucepan. Add to shallot and ignite, shaking pan gently until flame subsides. Drain liquid from morels into saucepan. Stir in cream. Cook until liquid is reduced by half. Blend in demi-glace and continue cooking until reduced by half. Add morels and season to taste with salt and pepper.

Transfer veal to large platter and serve immediately with sauce.

Veal Chops en Papillote with Leeks, Carrots, Parsnips and Spiced Butter

4 servings

Spiced Butter
2 1 × 1-inch pieces peeled fresh horseradish, squeezed dry *or* 2 tablespoons prepared, drained
¼ cup fresh parsley leaves
3 tablespoons unsalted butter, room temperature
1 tablespoon tarragon vinegar
1½ teaspoons fresh tarragon leaves *or* ⅛ teaspoon dried
¼ teaspoon coarse salt

¼ teaspoon freshly ground pepper

Vegetables
1 cup 3 × ⅛-inch julienne of leek
1 cup 3 × ⅛-inch julienne of parsnip
1 cup thinly sliced carrots, cut diagonally
1 tablespoon minced fresh parsley
4 ¾-inch-thick veal center loin chops, trimmed of all fat

For spiced butter: Finely chop fresh horseradish in processor using on/off turns. Add remaining ingredients and blend well. Divide into fourths.

For vegetables: Mix all ingredients and divide into 4 equal portions.

Tear off four 12 × 11-inch sheets of foil or parchment paper. Lightly sprinkle lower half of each with salt and pepper. Spread each with ⅓ of 1 vegetable portion. Top with veal. Spread each with half of 1 butter portion. Sprinkle lightly with salt. Top with remaining ⅔ of vegetable portion. Dot with remaining butter. Fold top half of foil or parchment over veal and vegetables. Make ½-inch fold with top and bottom edges and crease to seal. Repeat. Double-fold sides in same way. *(Can be prepared up to 12 hours ahead and refrigerated. Bring packets to room temperature before baking.)*

Preheat oven to 400°F. Arrange packets on baking sheet. Bake 20 minutes. Invert each to distribute liquid, then turn right side up. Serve immediately.

Veal Roulades with Wild Rice Stuffing and Mustard Sauce

6 servings

1⅔ cups water
6 tablespoons wild rice

3 tablespoons butter
3 tablespoons all purpose flour
3 cups hard cider, or more
1½ tablespoons Dijon mustard

6 tablespoons (¾ stick) unsalted butter
½ cup chopped onion

½ cup chopped seedless *or* seeded green grapes
Salt and freshly ground pepper

12 medium veal scallops (about 2 pounds total), pounded ¼ inch thick

2 tablespoons Calvados *or* applejack

½ cup chopped fresh parsley
Watercress sprigs (garnish)

Bring water to boil in heavy small saucepan. Stir in rice. Reduce heat to medium low, cover and simmer until rice is tender but still crunchy and water is absorbed, about 30 minutes.

Melt butter in heavy medium saucepan over medium-low heat. Add flour and stir 3 minutes. Gradually add 3 cups cider. Increase heat to medium high and stir until sauce boils and thickens enough to coat back of spoon (if sauce is too thick, add more cider). Remove from heat. Whisk in mustard. Taste and adjust seasoning.

Melt 2 tablespoons unsalted butter in heavy medium skillet over medium-high heat. Add onion and stir until soft but not brown, about 5 minutes. Let cool. Mix in rice, grapes and 1 tablespoon sauce. Season with salt and pepper.

Preheat oven to 350°F. Grease 8 × 12-inch baking dish. Place heaping tablespoon of stuffing in center of each veal scallop. Spread evenly, leaving small border. Roll veal up and tie securely. Melt remaining 4 tablespoons unsalted butter in heavy large skillet over medium-high heat. Add roulades and brown on all sides. Transfer roulades to baking dish. Discard fat from skillet. Deglaze pan with Calvados and pour over roulades. Top with sauce. Bake until veal is tender and juices run clear when roulade is pierced with skewer, 20 to 25 minutes.

Place 2 roulades in center of each individual plate. Spoon some sauce over roulade and top with parsley. Garnish with watercress. Serve remaining sauce separately.

Phyllo-wrapped Veal Roll

6 servings

2 tablespoons olive oil
1 medium onion, minced
1½ pounds ground veal
1 medium tomato, peeled, seeded and chopped
1 tablespoon chopped fresh thyme *or* 1 teaspoon dried
1 teaspoon cinnamon

4 tablespoons (½ stick) butter
3 tablespoons all purpose flour
1 cup milk
1 egg, beaten to blend, room temperature

¼ cup pine nuts (1¼ ounces)

2 tablespoons olive oil
1 garlic clove, minced
6 ounces stemmed fresh spinach, chopped (1 large bunch)
¼ teaspoon freshly grated nutmeg
Salt and freshly ground pepper

½ cup freshly grated Romano cheese

10 phyllo pastry sheets (do not use ultrathin)
⅓ cup unsalted butter, melted

Heat 2 tablespoons olive oil in heavy large skillet over medium-low heat. Add onion and cook until soft, about 10 minutes. Add meat and cook, breaking up with fork and spooning off excess liquid as it accumulates, until only a few traces of pink remain, 5 to 8 minutes. Add tomato, thyme and cinnamon. Cover and simmer 20 minutes, stirring occasionally.

Meanwhile, melt 3 tablespoons butter in heavy small saucepan over low heat. Add flour and stir 3 minutes. Pour in milk, increase heat to medium high and stir until sauce boils and thickens. Remove from heat. Whisk in egg. Place over medium heat and continue stirring 2 minutes. Set sauce aside.

Melt remaining 1 tablespoon butter in heavy small skillet over medium heat. Add pine nuts and stir until golden brown. Drain on paper towels.

Heat 2 tablespoons olive oil in heavy large skillet over medium-high heat. Add garlic and sauté just until it begins to release fragrance. Blend in spinach, cover and cook just until wilted, about 1 to 2 minutes. Season with nutmeg and salt and pepper.

Stir sauce, pine nuts and cheese into meat. Season with salt and pepper. Let cool. *(Can be prepared ahead to this point.)*

Preheat oven to 350°F. Lightly grease rimmed large baking sheet. Cover work surface with kitchen towel. Place 2 phyllo sheets on towel with long edge nearest you. Brush generously with melted butter. Repeat 4 more times, brushing each double layer with butter. Spread cooled meat mixture on phyllo, leaving 1¼-inch border. Arrange spinach in lengthwise strip along center of meat. Using towel as aid, roll phyllo up lengthwise. Transfer seam side down to prepared baking sheet. *(Can be assembled ahead and refrigerated overnight.)* Bake until crisp and golden, about 1 hour. Let roll stand for 10 to 15 minutes before slicing.

The Roof's Filet de Veau Brillat-Savarin

An elegant dish from The Roof restaurant in the Hotel Utah, Salt Lake City.

4 servings

6 to 8 tablespoons butter
8 3-ounce veal fillets (preferably milk-fed veal, cut from loin)
  Salt and freshly ground pepper

18 mushroom caps, thinly sliced
3 to 4 tablespoons chopped shallot

½ cup dry Sherry

8 10-inch crepes
  Butter, melted
½ cup grated Gruyère cheese
  or Mushroom sauce (use your favorite recipe)

Butter baking sheet and set aside. Melt 6 to 8 tablespoons butter in large skillet over medium-high heat. Add veal fillets in batches and sauté on both sides until nicely browned and almost cooked through, about 2 to 4 minutes. Season with salt and pepper. Remove veal from skillet; set aside and keep warm.

Add mushrooms and shallot to same skillet and sauté over medium-high heat, scraping up any browned bits clinging to bottom of pan, for 3 to 4 minutes. Add Sherry and continue cooking, stirring mixture constantly, until liquid is reduced, about 5 minutes.

Preheat oven to 400°F. Divide mixture evenly among crepes. Top each with veal fillet. Carefully fold crepe over meat. Brush each crepe on both sides with some of melted butter. Arrange seam side down on baking sheet. *(Can be prepared several hours ahead to this point and set aside at room temperature.)* Sprinkle top with cheese. Bake crepes until heated through, about 5 to 7 minutes. Serve hot. Serve sauce separately.

❦ *Braising and Poaching*

Braised Veal Chops in Tarragon Cream

Parslied pilaf is a good accompaniment. The tarragon cream can also be used as a sauce over tournedos or hamburgers.

4 to 6 servings

1 cup whipping cream
2 tablespoons minced fresh tarragon
1 tablespoon Dijon mustard

4 to 6 veal rib chops, cut ¾ inch thick
  Salt and freshly ground pepper
  All purpose flour
2 to 3 tablespoons butter

1 tablespoon vegetable oil
2 cups finely sliced onion
1 teaspoon minced garlic
¼ cup white wine vinegar
1 large fresh tarragon sprig
1 bay leaf
½ cup brown chicken stock

  Minced fresh parsley (garnish)

Position rack in center of oven and preheat to 325°F. Combine cream, minced tarragon and mustard and blend well; set aside.

Dry chops thoroughly with paper towels. Season with salt and pepper. Dredge lightly in flour, shaking off excess. Heat 2 tablespoons butter with a little oil in heavy 12-inch skillet over medium-high heat. Add chops 2 or 3 at a time and sauté until browned, about 2 to 3 minutes per side. Remove. If fat in skillet has burned, wipe out pan and add more butter and oil. Place over medium heat, add onion and garlic and sauté until onion is soft and browned, about 5 to 6 minutes;

do not burn. Season with salt and pepper. Add vinegar, tarragon sprig and bay leaf. Bring to simmer and let cook until vinegar is reduced by half. Return chops to skillet and add a little of stock. Cover and braise 25 minutes, adding stock about every 10 minutes and turning meat once.

Transfer chops to heated serving platter and keep warm. Discard tarragon sprig and bay leaf. Bring pan juices to simmer over direct heat, add cream mixture and cook until sauce is reduced and coats spoon heavily. Taste and adjust seasoning. Spoon over chops, sprinkle with parsley and serve immediately.

Wild Rice–stuffed Veal Birds

2 servings

⅓ to ⅔ cup chicken stock
2 tablespoons wild rice, rinsed thoroughly
¼ ounce dried mushrooms

2 large *or* 3 medium mushrooms (2 ounces)
1 tablespoon butter
2 tablespoons freshly grated Parmesan cheese
2 tablespoons minced fresh parsley

½ pound veal, cut evenly into 4 thin slices

1 tablespoon clarified butter
¾ cup beef stock
½ cup dry white wine
1 tablespoon minced shallot
1½ teaspoons minced fresh thyme *or* ½ teaspoon dried
1 tablespoon butter
Salt and freshly ground pepper

1 tablespoon butter
6 cherry tomatoes

Bring ⅓ cup Chicken Stock to boil in small saucepan over medium-high heat. Stir in wild rice. Reduce heat to very low, cover and simmer until tender, about 45 to 50 minutes, adding more stock as necessary. Meanwhile, combine dried mushrooms with enough warm water to cover. Let mushrooms soften about 30 minutes.

Remove soaked mushrooms with slotted spoon; discard water. Pat mushrooms dry. Trim away hard stems and discard. Finely chop both dried and fresh mushrooms. Melt 1 tablespoon butter in small skillet over medium heat. Add mushrooms and cook until tender and liquid has evaporated, about 3 to 4 minutes. Reserve skillet; do not clean. Drain any excess stock from cooked rice. Add mushrooms, cheese and 1 tablespoon parsley to rice.

Pound veal slices lightly until very thin. Spoon ¼ of wild rice mixture onto each veal scallop. Roll up and secure with toothpicks or heavy thread. Heat clarified butter in reserved skillet over medium-high heat. Add veal and brown well on all sides, 5 to 6 minutes total. Add ¼ cup beef stock with wine, shallot, thyme and remaining 1 tablespoon parsley and bring to boil. Reduce heat to low, cover and simmer very gently until veal is cooked, about 15 minutes. Transfer veal to platter and keep warm. Add remaining ½ cup beef stock to skillet, increase heat to high and boil until reduced by half, scraping up any browned bits. Whisk in 1 tablespoon butter. Season to taste with salt and pepper. Pour sauce over veal.

Melt 1 tablespoon butter in small skillet over medium-high heat. Add cherry tomatoes and sauté until heated through, turning frequently. Season with salt and pepper. Garnish veal with tomatoes and serve.

Veal Ragout with Onions and Chestnuts

A light but richly flavored main course that is just right for an informal dinner party or a festive family supper. Start with a spinach, mushroom and water chestnut crepe. An ideal dessert would be poached pears in chocolate sabayon. Suggested wine: A dry Chenin Blanc.

6 to 8 servings

5 tablespoons (about) unsalted butter
4 tablespoons (about) chicken fat *or* vegetable oil
3 pounds boned veal shoulder, trimmed and cut into 1½-inch cubes
Salt and freshly ground white pepper

All purpose flour
2¼ cups brown chicken stock
16 garlic cloves
2 small yellow onions

1 large sprig fresh thyme *or* 1 teaspoon dried

2 tablespoons chicken fat *or* vegetable oil
1 tablespoon firmly packed brown sugar
16 to 18 fresh *or* frozen tiny white onions
16 to 18 peeled fresh chestnuts

1 cup whipping cream
Beurre manié (optional)*
Minced fresh parsley (garnish)

Heat 2 tablespoons unsalted butter with 1 tablespoon fat in heavy large ovenproof casserole over medium-high heat. Add veal in batches *(do not crowd)* and sauté until nicely browned on all sides, adding more butter and fat as necessary. Return all veal to casserole and season to taste with salt and pepper.

Position rack in center of oven and preheat to 350°F. Sprinkle veal with flour and toss until veal is covered and lightly glazed. Add about 1¾ cups stock, garlic, yellow onions and thyme and blend well. Bring to boil over medium-high heat, stirring frequently to prevent sticking. Cover and bake until meat is tender, about 1½ hours.

Meanwhile, heat 2 tablespoons fat and brown sugar in heavy large skillet over medium-high heat. Add white onions and sauté until nicely browned. Add chestnuts and remaining stock. Reduce heat, cover partially and simmer until tender, about 15 minutes. Remove from heat and set aside.

When veal is done, remove from casserole using slotted spoon. Transfer pan juices with garlic to processor or blender and puree until smooth. Return puree to casserole. Stir in cream and chestnut mixture and bring to boil over medium-high heat. If sauce seems too thin, whisk in beurre manié a bit at a time and cook until sauce coats spoon. Add meat and heat through. Turn into dish or tureen and sprinkle with minced fresh parsley.

* 1 tablespoon softened unsalted butter mixed with 1 tablespoon sifted all purpose flour.

Veal with Pesto and Orzo
(Vitello al Pesto con Orzo)

8 servings

Parsley Pesto
½ cup walnuts
½ cup (packed) parsley sprigs
¼ cup freshly grated Parmesan cheese
¼ cup olive oil
1 teaspoon dried basil
1 teaspoon fresh lemon juice
3 large garlic cloves
   Freshly ground pepper

1 3- to 4-pound boneless veal shoulder roast
   Olive oil (for roast)
   Salt and freshly ground pepper

2 tablespoons (¼ stick) butter

2 medium onions, diced
2 carrots, thinly sliced
2 strips fresh pork fat *or* blanched bacon
½ cup dry white wine
½ cup chicken stock

4 Italian plum tomatoes, diced
½ cup dry white wine
½ cup chicken stock

1 pound orzo,* cooked al dente and drained
¼ cup chopped fresh parsley
   Freshly grated Parmesan cheese (optional)

For parsley pesto: Combine first 8 ingredients in processor and blend well. Set aside 2 tablespoons pesto (for orzo).

Preheat broiler. Spread top side of roast with remaining pesto. Roll roast up lengthwise and tie with string every 2 inches. Brush with olive oil and season with salt and pepper. Brown on all sides, about 2 inches from heat source, turning often. Set aside.

Preheat oven to 325°F. Melt butter in shallow flameproof casserole over medium heat. Add onions and carrots and sauté until onions are soft, about 7 minutes. Transfer roast to casserole, spooning vegetables over top. Cover roast with pork fat. Pour ½ cup wine and ½ cup chicken stock into casserole and bring to boil over medium-high heat. Cover tightly with aluminum foil. Top casserole with lid and bake until meat thermometer inserted in thickest portion of roast registers 175°F, about 1¾ to 2 hours. Transfer meat to serving platter and keep warm.

Skim fat from sauce. Add tomatoes, remaining ½ cup wine and ½ cup chicken stock to casserole and mix well. Bring to boil over medium-high heat. Reduce heat to medium and simmer until sauce thickens, about 8 to 10 minutes. Adjust seasonings to taste. Remove 1 cup sauce and keep warm.

Add reserved pesto, orzo and parsley to casserole and blend well over medium heat. Adjust seasonings to taste. Spoon orzo mixture around roast. Carve roast into ¾-inch-thick slices. Serve immediately with reserved sauce. Serve Parmesan cheese separately.

*Orzo is rice-shaped pasta available in Italian or Middle Eastern food markets.

Stuffed Breast of Veal (Cima alla Genovese)

This is the easiest form of galantine (a stuffed, cooked meat roll).

12 servings

Stuffing
1 pair veal sweetbreads
1 teaspoon salt

1 pair calf's brains
6 cups water
2 tablespoons vinegar
1 teaspoon salt

4 eggs
½ cup freshly grated Parmesan cheese
1 medium garlic clove, minced
1 teaspoon minced fresh marjoram *or* ¼ teaspoon dried
½ teaspoon salt
¼ teaspoon freshly ground pepper
Freshly grated nutmeg
2 bunches (about 2 pounds) fresh spinach, stems removed, washed, blanched, drained, squeezed dry and finely chopped

1 cup uncooked fresh peas *or* barely thawed frozen peas
¼ cup pine nuts (optional)
¼ cup skinned pistachios (optional)

1 6- to 7-pound breast of milk-fed veal (have butcher bone, trim well and make pocket at 1 end)
2 hard-cooked eggs
1 carrot, parboiled until tender and cut into large julienne

4 celery stalks, cut into thirds
3 carrots, peeled and quartered
1 large onion, cut into chunks
Parsley sprigs, tied in a bunch
8 cups water

For stuffing: Soak sweetbreads 3 hours in enough cold water to cover, changing water several times. Drain well. Peel off membrane. Transfer sweetbreads to small saucepan, cover with cold water and add salt. Place over medium-low heat and bring to boil. Reduce heat and simmer 5 minutes. Plunge sweetbreads into cold water; drain well. Transfer to plate, cover with another plate and weight with cans or other heavy objects. Let cool completely. Cut into julienne slices.

Wash brains thoroughly. Peel off membrane. Soak brains 3 hours in enough cold water to cover, changing water every 20 minutes. Drain well. Transfer to medium saucepan. Add 6 cups water, vinegar and salt. Place over medium-high heat and bring to boil. Reduce heat and simmer 25 minutes. Remove from heat and let cool completely in cooking liquid. Drain well. Transfer to plate, cover with another plate and weight with heavy objects until liquid no longer exudes and brains are firm, about 1 hour.

Beat eggs in large bowl. Add cheese, garlic, marjoram, salt, pepper and nutmeg and blend well. Add spinach, peas and nuts. Adjust seasoning.

Fill veal pocket with ¾ of stuffing, being careful not to tear skin. Push hard-cooked eggs into center of stuffing; then poke carrot, sweetbreads and brains into filling around eggs. Fill with remaining stuffing. Sew pocket closed. Turn veal over twice to distribute filling evenly. Wrap with cheesecloth and tie securely so meat will retain its shape while cooking.

Make bed of celery, carrots, onion and parsley in bottom of pot or roasting pan just large enough to accommodate veal. Set veal on top. Add water. Bring to boil over medium-high heat, skimming foam as it accumulates on surface. Reduce heat, cover partially and simmer 2 hours, turning veal every 30 minutes. Transfer veal to large platter (save stock for another use). Discard cheesecloth. Cover veal with large platter and weight with cans or other heavy objects. Let cool completely before slicing and serving.

Fresh Pasta

4 to 6 servings

3 egg yolks
2 eggs
2 tablespoons whipping cream
1 teaspoon salt
3 cups all purpose flour

Butter, room temperature

Butter (for skillet)
Salt

Whisk egg yolks, eggs, cream and salt in large bowl. Mix in flour until dough leaves sides of bowl. Form into ball. Turn out onto lightly floured surface and knead about 10 minutes. Coat with softened butter to prevent drying. Cover and refrigerate 2 hours.

Roll dough out on lightly floured work surface until paper thin and translucent, stretching and sprinkling with additional flour to prevent sticking. Let dry for 30 minutes.

Roll dough up lengthwise and slice into thin strips. Unroll into rapidly boiling salted water and cook until al dente, about 3 to 4 minutes. Remove from heat and drain well. Rinse in cold water and drain again. Melt butter in large skillet over medium heat. Add pasta and toss until heated through. Season with salt to taste.

Sweetbread Fettuccine with Ginger and Hazelnut Sauce

6 servings

1 pound veal sweetbreads
1½ teaspoons salt

2 tablespoons (½ stick) unsalted butter
½ cup diced onion
½ cup diced carrot
½ cup diced leek (white part only)
½ cup chopped white mushrooms
¼ cup diced celery
1 bay leaf
1 fresh thyme sprig *or* pinch of dried

Salt and freshly ground pepper

1 tablespoon unsalted butter
2 tablespoons diced shallot
2½ cups Chardonnay
¼ cup hazelnuts, blanched, drained, peeled and chopped
2 cups whipping cream
2 tablespoons chopped fresh ginger

1 pound fettuccine, cooked al dente
¼ cup (½ stick) unsalted butter, room temperature

Combine sweetbreads, ½ teaspoon salt and enough cold water to cover in large bowl. Soak overnight in refrigerator, changing salted water twice. Drain sweetbreads and transfer to large saucepan. Add cold water to cover by 2 inches. Bring to simmer and cook 5 minutes. Drain sweetbreads, reserving 2½ cups stock. Rinse sweetbreads under cold water. Peel off thin membrane and discard. Set sweetbreads aside.

Melt 2 tablespoons butter in heavy 10-inch skillet over low heat. Add onion, carrot, leek, mushrooms and celery and sauté just until softened. Add sweetbreads and reserved stock to skillet. Add bay leaf, thyme and salt and pepper. Cover and cook over low heat until sweetbreads are tender, turning once, about 45 minutes. Transfer to platter using slotted spoon; keep warm. Strain and degrease stock, pressing gently on solids with back of spoon to extract liquid. Return stock to skillet; reduce by half over high heat.

Melt 1 tablespoon butter in medium saucepan over medium heat. Add shallot and sauté until translucent. Add wine. Increase heat to high and reduce until almost dry, adding chopped hazelnuts halfway through reduction. Add reduced stock and cream. Reduce again by half. Strain sauce and return to saucepan over low heat. Stir in ginger and cook 2 minutes. Adjust seasoning. Strain again.

Toss fettuccine with ¼ cup butter. Arrange on platter. Thinly slice sweetbreads and arrange over fettuccine. Pour sauce over and serve.

Savory Veal One-pot (Eingemachtes Kalbfleisch)

4 to 5 servings

1¾ pounds veal stew meat (cut from shoulder *or* breast), trimmed and cut into 1¼-inch cubes
2 tablespoons (¼ stick) butter
1 small onion, finely chopped
¾ cup water
7 to 8 peppercorns, finely crushed
3 ¼-inch-thick strips lemon peel
1 small bay leaf
½ teaspoon salt
Pinch of sugar

3 tablespoons butter
½ pound small mushrooms, trimmed
3 leeks (include some of green), cut into ¾-inch lengths

1 cup cauliflower florets

Sauce
1 tablespoon butter
1 tablespoon all purpose flour
1 egg yolk, lightly beaten
2 tablespoons whipping cream
1 tablespoon chopped capers, rinsed and drained
Juice of ½ lemon
Salt

1½ teaspoons chopped fresh parsley (garnish)
Lemon wedges (garnish)

Combine veal in 3-quart Dutch oven or flameproof casserole with enough water to cover. Place over medium heat and bring to boil. Let boil 5 minutes. Drain veal well. Rinse out Dutch oven and return to medium heat. Add 2 tablespoons butter and stir until melted. Blend in onion and cook 3 to 4 minutes. Add ¾ cup water and veal. Stir in peppercorns, lemon peel, bay leaf, salt and sugar and bring to boil. Reduce heat to low; cover and simmer 1 hour.

Melt 3 tablespoons butter in medium skillet over medium-high heat. Add mushrooms and cook 3 to 4 minutes; set aside (do not wipe out skillet). Remove lemon peel and bay leaf from stock and discard. Layer mushrooms, leeks and cauliflower florets in Dutch oven. Cover and cook until vegetables are tender, about 15 minutes.

For sauce: About 5 minutes before vegetables are done, melt 1 tablespoon butter in same skillet over medium heat. Stir in flour and mix until smooth. Cook about 2 minutes. Gradually drain stock from Dutch oven into flour mixture and stir until sauce is smooth. Combine egg yolk and cream in small bowl. Slowly stir ¼ cup sauce into egg mixture. Gradually add egg mixture to sauce, stirring constantly. Mix in capers and lemon juice. Remove from heat. Season to taste with salt. Transfer veal and vegetables to serving dish. Pour sauce over top. Garnish with chopped parsley and lemon wedges and serve immediately.

Veal and Sorrel Stew in Gougère Ring

6 to 8 servings

2 cups Gewürztraminer *or* dry white wine
2 cups water
1 onion, stuck with 2 whole cloves
1 bouquet garni (sliced leek, parsley, thyme, bay leaf and garlic clove, tied together in a cheesecloth bag)
1½ pounds veal stew meat, cut into 1-inch cubes
1½ pounds boneless pork, cut into 1-inch cubes

1 tablespoon butter

¼ pound sorrel, stemmed
3 tablespoons butter
3 tablespoons all purpose flour

½ cup whipping cream
2 egg yolks
 Salt and freshly ground pepper
 Gougère Ring (see following recipe)
 Fresh sorrel chiffonade (optional garnish)

Combine wine, water, onion and bouquet garni in Dutch oven or large casserole and bring to boil over medium-high heat. Reduce heat and add veal and pork. Cover and simmer very gently until veal and pork are tender when pierced, about 1½ hours.

Melt 1 tablespoon butter in small skillet. Add sorrel and cook over low heat until very soft. Puree with back of spoon. Set aside to cool.

Remove meat from stock using slotted spoon. Discard bouquet garni. Melt 3 tablespoons butter in large saucepan over low heat. Stir in flour and cook until roux is pale gold. Add stock and bring to boil. Reduce heat to low and simmer until slightly thickened, about 20 minutes, stirring occasionally.

Combine cream and egg yolks in large bowl and whisk thoroughly. Stir about ¼ cup warm sauce into cream mixture. Slowly pour cream mixture into sauce, whisking well. Return meat to sauce and simmer gently until heated through. Stir in reserved sorrel puree, blending well. Season stew with salt and pepper to taste. Spoon stew into center of Gougère Ring. Garnish with sorrel chiffonade.

Gougère Ring

6 to 8 servings

1 cup water
½ cup (1 stick) butter, cut into ½-inch pieces
1 cup sifted all purpose flour
 Pinch of salt

4 to 5 eggs
¾ cup diced Gruyère cheese

1 egg yolk beaten with 1 tablespoon water

Preheat oven to 425°F. Combine water and butter in large saucepan and bring to rapid boil over high heat. Remove from heat. Immediately stir in flour and salt. Place over medium heat and beat vigorously until dough pulls away from sides of pan and films bottom. Cool mixture for 5 minutes. Add eggs one at a time, beating well after each addition, until mixture is glossy and smooth. Stir in Gruyère, blending well.

Dampen baking sheet with cold water, shaking off excess (this will help pastry rise). Arrange large spoonfuls of dough next to each other in wreath pattern on sheet. Brush top with egg yolk mixture, being careful not to drip it on side. Bake 15 minutes. Reduce oven temperature to 375°F and bake until puffed and brown, about 15 more minutes. Slit gougère several places on side and return to turned-off oven with door ajar for 15 minutes to dry. Serve hot or at room temperature.

Rosy Calf's Liver with Lemon-Onion Marmalade

2 servings

2 3-ounce slices calf's liver (½ inch thick)
¼ teaspoon dried sage leaves
   Salt and freshly ground pepper
2 teaspoons olive oil

¼ cup dry Marsala *or* Sherry
2 teaspoons unsalted butter, well chilled

¼ teaspoon crushed black peppercorns *or* 1½ teaspoons crushed green peppercorns
4 fresh sage leaves
   Lemon-Onion Marmalade (see following recipe)
   Fresh watercress *or* parsley sprigs

Pat liver slices dry. Season both sides with dried sage and salt and pepper. Heat oil in heavy or nonstick large skillet over high heat. Add liver and sear quickly until outside is crusty but inside is still pink, about 2 to 3 minutes. Transfer to heated individual plates.

Return skillet to medium-high heat. Add Marsala and cook until reduced by half, scraping up any browned bits. Swirl in butter and crushed peppercorns and cook until bubbly. Pour sauce over liver. Garnish each slice with fresh sage leaf. Divide marmalade evenly between plates. Top marmalade with watercress sprigs.

Lemon-Onion Marmalade

2 servings

2 teaspoons olive oil
2 cups coarsely chopped onion
1 unpeeled lemon, coarsely chopped and seeded (about ⅔ cup)

2 teaspoons sugar
2 teaspoons Sherry wine vinegar

Heat oil in heavy or nonstick medium skillet over medium-high heat. Add onion and lemon and cook 3 to 4 minutes. Sprinkle with sugar. Cover partially, reduce heat to low and cook until onion and lemon are softened and glossy, stirring occasionally. Blend in vinegar and continue cooking until mixture is reduced to coarse puree, 30 to 40 minutes total. Serve warm.

Crisp Liver in Lemon Sauce

2 servings

6 slices bacon

¼ cup all purpose flour
2 teaspoons dried dillweed
½ teaspoon salt
¼ teaspoon freshly ground pepper
½ pound calf's *or* beef liver, cut into bite-size pieces

3 tablespoons butter
2 tablespoons fresh lemon juice
1 tablespoon minced fresh parsley
1 tablespoon grated lemon peel (garnish)

Cook bacon in heavy large skillet over medium-high heat until crisp. Drain on paper towels (do not clean skillet). Crumble bacon and set aside.

Combine flour, dillweed, salt and pepper in paper bag. Add liver and coat well, shaking off any excess flour mixture. Place same skillet over high heat. Add liver and sauté until crisp on outside but still moist and pink inside, about 4 to 6 minutes. Remove liver and keep warm. Discard fat from skillet. Reduce heat to medium and add butter to skillet, scraping up any browned bits. Stir in lemon juice, parsley and crumbled bacon. Pour over liver. Garnish with grated lemon peel and serve.

3 ❦ Lamb

Lamb is an elemental part of human celebration. Roast lamb is the centerpiece of the Easter and Passover feasts. In Arab countries, it is the height of hospitality for honored guests, an inseparable part of life's most special moments. The ancient Chinese *Book of Songs* sang the praises of its aroma: "God on high is much pleased." The world over, lamb is a symbol of rebirth, of spring in all its freshness.

In no part of the world is lamb more popular than in the Middle East and the Mediterranean, and this chapter highlights recipes from both regions. The Middle Eastern love of sweet and aromatic ingredients in savory dishes is reflected in Moroccan Lamb Tajine with Dates (page 83), and Lamb Pastitsio (page 78). Greek dishes such as Stuffed Leg of Lamb Wrapped in Pastry (page 71), Ragout of Lamb à la Grecque (page 82) and Lamb Tart Avgolemono (page 81) are redolent of the garlic, herbs and spices that make the cuisine so distinctive. And the tomatoes, garlic, onions and bounteous herbs of Southern France impart their character to such recipes as Lamb Shanks Provençal (page 86), Rack of Lamb Moutarde (page 77) and Miniature Lamb Patties with Sauce Basquaise (page 68).

As these recipes suggest, lamb's unique flavor—sweet and delicate, yet ever-so-slightly musky—suits it to all manner of seasonings and cooking treatments. You'll also find here spicy curries of lamb from India, quick and pungently seasoned stir-fries from China, a Yorkshire Deviled Shoulder of Lamb from England (page 74), and plenty of satisfying recipes from much closer to home.

To ensure success with whichever recipe you select, freshness is essential; lamb's flavor and tenderness will be at its peak if the meat is cooked on the day of purchase. If you're lucky enough to find it, get baby lamb or milk lamb, the incomparably tender meat of animals no more than ten weeks old. Most lamb for sale, though, is spring lamb, six months to a year old, and it should have the firm, deep pink flesh, moist white fat, and soft, porous bones that indicate high-quality meat.

🌣 Grilling and Broiling

Apricot-stuffed Lamb Chops

2 servings

4 dried apricots, halved
2 tablespoons thinly slivered onion
2 double-thick (2 ribs each) lamb loin chops (about 8 ounces each), pocket cut horizontally through center to bone
¼ cup parsley sprigs
2 teaspoons olive oil

1 teaspoon Herbes de Provence
1 garlic clove
2 to 3 tablespoons fresh lemon juice
Grated peel of 1 lemon

Fresh mint sprigs and lemon wedges (optional garnishes)

Insert 4 apricot halves and 1 tablespoon slivered onion into pocket of each lamb chop. Press firmly to close. Mix parsley, olive oil, Herbes de Provence, garlic, lemon juice and peel in processor to coarse paste. Rub evenly over both sides of each chop. Cover and set aside at room temperature 2 hours.

Grease broiler pan and set about 5 inches from heat source. Preheat broiler. Transfer lamb chops to heated pan. Broil until chops are crusty and brown outside but still pink inside, about 7 minutes on each side. Transfer to individual plates. Garnish with mint sprigs and lemon and serve.

Lamb Chops with Pine Nuts

2 servings

4 tablespoons pine nuts
¼ cup tomato paste
2 garlic cloves, chopped
1 dried hot red chili (about 1 inch long), stemmed, seeded, soaked, drained and chopped
1 tablespoon vinegar

½ teaspoon sugar
¼ teaspoon salt
6 tablespoons olive oil

4 small lamb loin chops *or* 2 ground lamb patties

Heat pine nuts in small ungreased skillet over medium heat until pale golden brown. Set aside 2 tablespoons nuts; transfer remainder to processor or blender. Add tomato paste, garlic, chili, vinegar, sugar and salt and mix well. With machine running, slowly add olive oil in thin stream and continue mixing until thick and well blended. *(Can be prepared early in the day and refrigerated. Mix briefly to recombine just before using.)*

Arrange lamb chops on lightly oiled broiler pan and spread about 1 tablespoon sauce on each. Broil about 5 minutes; turn meat, coat other side with sauce and continue broiling to desired doneness. (Lamb can also be prepared on barbecue grill. Brush with sauce during cooking.) Transfer to heated plates, sprinkle with reserved nuts and serve with any remaining sauce.

🌣

Skewered Barbecued Lamb (Saté Kambing)

Makes about 12 skewers

3 large green onions, minced
1 large garlic clove, minced
½ cup Indonesian Soy Sauce (see recipe, page 89) *or* commercial kecap manis
1 tablespoon fresh lemon juice
½ teaspoon crushed chili paste

(sambal oelek), dried red pepper flakes *or* chili powder
1 pound boneless lean lamb shoulder, cut into ½-inch cubes
    Peanut Sauce (kacang saus) (see recipe, page 89)

Combine onions, garlic, soy sauce, lemon juice and chili paste in bowl. Add lamb and mix well. Cover and marinate 1 hour, tossing frequently. Thread on skewers. Broil, turning and basting, about 5 minutes, or until done. Serve with Peanut Sauce.

Shish Kebab

Leg of lamb varies in size; as a rule of thumb, plan on ½ pound per serving before boning and trimming.

8 to 10 servings

1 large onion, minced
½ to ¾ cup minced fresh parsley
½ to 1 cup vegetable oil
½ to 1 cup dry red wine
2 to 3 garlic cloves, minced
    Garlic salt and freshly ground pepper
3 pounds boned, trimmed leg of lamb, cut into 2- to 2½-inch cubes

1 large onion, cut into 8 to 10 pieces
1 large green bell pepper, cut into 8 to 10 pieces
8 to 10 large mushrooms
    Salt

Combine minced onion, parsley, oil, wine, garlic and salt and pepper in glass bowl. Add meat and stir to coat well. Cover and refrigerate overnight.

Prepare barbecue or preheat broiler. Drain meat. Alternate on skewer with 1 piece onion, 1 piece green pepper and 1 mushroom. Grill or broil to desired doneness. Salt just before serving.

Butterflied Lamb in the Style of the South

"The South," in this case, is the southwestern area of France, where this seasoning combination supposedly originated. As the lamb cooks, add herbs drained from the marinade to the fire to create an enticing aroma.

6 to 8 servings

1 750-ml bottle Beaujolais
¼ cup olive oil
16 sprigs fresh rosemary, lightly bruised, *or* 2 tablespoons dried
12 branches fresh thyme, lightly bruised, *or* 2 teaspoons dried
3 garlic cloves, lightly crushed

1 branch fresh sage, lightly bruised, *or* ¼ teaspoon dried
1 teaspoon coarsely ground pepper
    Salt
1 6- to 7-pound leg of lamb, boned and butterflied

Combine all ingredients except meat in large bowl and blend well. Set lamb in large shallow dish and pour marinade over. Cover and refrigerate 24 hours, turning at least once. Drain marinade into bowl. Pat meat dry.

Heat coals until gray ash forms. Spread into overlapping layer and let burn 30 minutes. Set grill 4 inches above coals; let coals burn until moderately hot. Place lamb flat on grill and cook, brushing occasionally with marinade and adding coals to fire if necessary, until meat thermometer inserted in thickest part registers desired degree of doneness, about 135°F for medium rare (about 20 minutes per side). Let stand about 10 minutes, then slice thinly.

❦ Sautéing and Stir-frying

Lamb Noisettes with Garlic Soubise in Artichokes

The classic onion puree, soubise, is regally combined here with a head of garlic that adds unexpected subtlety to this sauce for lamb fillets. Sautéed eggplant slices or broiled tomatoes can be used instead of artichokes.

4 servings

1 head garlic

2 tablespoons (¼ stick) butter
2 tablespoons olive oil
3 large (about 1½ pounds) onions, diced

2 tablespoons all purpose flour
2 cups milk
½ cup whipping cream *or* lamb stock
⅛ teaspoon freshly grated nutmeg

Salt and freshly ground pepper

8 large artichokes
1 lemon, halved
¼ cup (½ stick) butter

8 lamb loin chops
2 tablespoons (¼ stick) butter
2 tablespoons olive oil

½ cup Madeira

Separate garlic into individual cloves. Blanch 3 minutes in pan of boiling water. Drain and peel.

Heat 2 tablespoons butter and 2 tablespoons oil in large heavy saucepan over low heat. Add onions and garlic, cover and cook until vegetables are tender and translucent, about 30 minutes, stirring occasionally.

Whisk in flour and let mixture foam over low heat 3 minutes without coloring, stirring constantly. Whisk in milk and stir over medium-high heat until sauce comes to boil. Reduce heat and simmer until reduced by half, about 1 hour, stirring occasionally. Puree in blender or processor, stopping as necessary to scrape down sides of container. Mix in cream. Season with nutmeg and salt and pepper. Keep sauce warm in double boiler.

Slice off stems of artichokes at base to leave smooth bottoms. Remove any tough or discolored bottom leaves. Cut off about an inch or so of top leaves. Rub base and all cut portions of artichoke with half a lemon. Steam artichokes until tender and easily pierced with knife, about 20 to 30 minutes. Drain and cool on rack. Scoop out chokes. Melt butter in gratin dish or deep serving platter. Add artichokes and coat well. Arrange choke side up and sprinkle with salt and pepper. Keep warm in low oven. *(Artichokes can be prepared several days ahead. Dot with butter and reheat in covered dish about 15 minutes at 325°F.)*

Bone chops, remove gristle and fat, and trim into neat round noisettes. Pat dry with paper towels. Heat 2 tablespoons butter and 2 tablespoons olive oil in large heavy skillet over medium-high heat. Add meat and sauté 5 minutes, turning once. Season both sides with salt and pepper to taste. Arrange each noisette in artichoke and return to warm oven.

Pour off fat from skillet. Add Madeira and deglaze over high heat until liquid is reduced to several tablespoons, scraping up any browned bits clinging to bottom of pan. Blend into warm sauce. Taste and adjust seasoning. Spoon over meat and serve immediately.

Lamb Scallops with Fennel
(Escalopes de Gigot d'Agneau au Fenouil)

6 to 8 servings

¼ pound dried red beans
3 cups water

Lamb Scallops
1 4-pound leg of lamb, tail and hip bones removed

½ cup minced fresh parsley
2 large shallots, minced
1 teaspoon minced fresh savory *or* ½ teaspoon dried, ground

2 cups 1-inch cubes crustless day-old French bread
2 teaspoons fennel seed, crushed
¼ teaspoon salt
   Freshly ground pepper

Sauce
1 tablespoon unsalted butter
2½ cups veal stock

2 eggs

2 teaspoons corn oil
2 teaspoons water
½ teaspoon salt
¼ cup all purpose flour

Vegetables
3 tablespoons unsalted butter
1 large onion, sliced into ½-inch-thick rings
4 2-inch-wide fennel bulbs (discard tough outer ribs), halved lengthwise and cored

10 tablespoons clarified butter
2 large garlic cloves, thinly sliced
2 tablespoons minced fennel fronds
1 tablespoon butter
12 cherry tomatoes, sautéed in butter (garnish)
   Watercress (garnish)

Soak beans in 3 cups water overnight. Bring mixture to boil in heavy medium saucepan and simmer until tender, about 3 hours. Drain well.

For lamb scallops: Peel fell from lamb. Place lamb on work surface with bone on top. Cut from rounded bone end along bone to joint, then down length of shank to end, using small sharp knife, to expose bone. Cut around bone to free it, slanting knife tip as close to bone as possible. Separate meat along natural divisions. Cut wide pieces of meat into ⅓-inch-thick scallops. Cut narrow shank meat into ½-inch cubes; reserve cubes. Pound each scallop *once* to flatten.

Mix parsley, shallots and savory. Press mixture into both sides of scallops. Cover and refrigerate 3 to 4 hours.

Grind bread into fine crumbs in processor or blender. Blend in fennel seed, ¼ teaspoon salt and pepper. Spread out onto large plate. Let stand at room temperature until dry, about 1 hour.

For sauce: Heat 1 tablespoon butter in heavy large skillet over medium-high heat. Add reserved lamb cubes and brown well on all sides. Add stock, reduce heat and simmer until liquid is reduced to ⅔ cup, about 1½ hours. Strain through fine sieve into clean saucepan and set aside.

Beat eggs, oil, water and ½ teaspoon salt in small bowl. Season to taste with pepper. Flour lamb scallops very lightly, patting off excess. Brush with egg mixture, then coat as lightly as possible with breadcrumbs. Set on wire rack to dry at room temperature 1 hour.

For vegetables: Melt 3 tablespoons butter in heavy large skillet over medium-low heat. Add onion, cover and cook until translucent. Cut fennel crosswise into ¼-inch-thick slices. Add to onion and cook, stirring, until crisp-tender, 3 to 4 minutes. Stir in red beans and season with salt and pepper.

Heat clarified butter in heavy large skillet over low heat. Add garlic and cook until just golden. Remove garlic and reserve. Increase heat to medium high. When butter is very hot, quickly brown lamb in batches until golden on both sides, about 2 minutes total for rare. Arrange on large oval platter. Meanwhile, reheat bean mixture, spoon around meat and sprinkle with fennel fronds. Sprinkle garlic over meat. Warm sauce over high heat. Stir in 1 tablespoon butter. Pour thin stream of sauce down center of lamb. Garnish with tomatoes and watercress. Serve immediately. Serve remaining sauce separately.

Lamb with Wild Mushroom Sauce

6 servings

8 dried morels
8 dried cèpes
2 cups warm water

1 tablespoon vegetable oil
11 ounces lamb bones and trimmings
¼ pound lamb stew meat
5¼ cups veal stock, heated

2 tablespoons (¼ stick) unsalted butter

1 tablespoon chopped shallot

6 tablespoons (¾ stick) unsalted butter
1 double lamb loin (about 3¼ pounds), cut into medallions
Salt and freshly ground pepper

Fresh lemon juice
1 tablespoons whipping cream
1 teaspoon unsalted butter

Soak morels and cèpes separately in 1 cup warm water 30 minutes. Strain morel liquid through several layers of moistened cheesecloth and reserve. Discard cèpe liquid. Rinse morels and cèpes separately in strainer under cold running water until all grit is removed; remove any twigs. Slice morels thinly; discard stems. Set mushrooms aside.

Heat oil in heavy large skillet over medium-high heat. Brown lamb bones and trimmings and stewing meat on all sides, turning occasionally. Remove bones, trimmings and stew meat; pour off fat. Add 1 cup hot stock to skillet, stirring to scrape up any browned bits. Add 4 cups hot stock and continue cooking, whisking occasionally.

Melt 2 tablespoons butter in heavy small skillet over medium-high heat. Add morels, cèpes and shallot and toss 2 minutes. Add to reducing stock with reserved morel liquid. Reduce heat to medium and continue cooking until sauce is reduced to 1 cup.

Meanwhile, melt 3 tablespoons butter in each of 2 heavy medium skillets over medium-high heat. Brown lamb medallions on both sides. Reduce heat slightly and cook to desired doneness, about 5 minutes total for medium rare. Season with salt and pepper. Deglaze skillets with remaining ¼ cup stock and add liquid to sauce.

Taste sauce and adjust seasoning with salt, pepper and lemon juice (be careful not to mask smoky flavor). Whisk in cream. Remove from heat and stir in remaining 1 teaspoon butter. Arrange lamb on plates. Top with some sauce. Serve remaining sauce separately.

Lamb Scallops with Linguine

2 servings

1 pound lamb slices, ⅜ to ½ inch thick, cut from leg
Salt and freshly ground pepper

2 large red bell peppers *or* 1 large red and 1 large yellow bell pepper

¼ cup olive oil
½ small yellow onion, sliced into thin rings

2 large garlic cloves, minced
1 teaspoon dried rosemary

2 tablespoons Burgundy

¼ pound spinach linguine, cooked al dente

¼ pound linguine, cooked al dente

Pound lamb slices to uniform thickness. Season with salt and pepper.

Char peppers over gas flame or under broiler until skins blister and blacken. Place in plastic bag, seal tightly and let steam 10 minutes. Peel skins and remove seeds. Cut peppers lengthwise into ⅜-inch strips. Set aside.

Heat oil in heavy large skillet over medium-high heat. Reduce heat to low, add onion, garlic and rosemary and stir to combine well. Cover and cook until tender, stirring frequently, 10 to 15 minutes. Remove onion mixture with slotted spoon and set aside.

Return skillet to medium-high heat. Add lamb and sauté until medium rare, about 1 minute per side. Remove lamb. Strain oil into clean large skillet. Add Burgundy to skillet used to sauté lamb and stir, scraping up any browned bits. Cook until syrupy, about 1 minute. Return lamb to skillet, turning in sauce to coat evenly. Remove from heat; keep warm.

Place skillet with strained oil over medium-high heat. Add onion mixture and peppers and toss just until heated. Arrange lamb on linguine. Spoon bell pepper mixture over.

Lamb with Artichokes and Lemon

6 servings

2½ pounds boned leg of lamb (about 5 pounds with bone), cut into 1½-inch cubes
Salt and freshly ground pepper
Ground oregano

3 tablespoons olive oil, or more
6 garlic cloves, minced

2 tablespoons fresh lemon juice
½ cup lamb *or* beef stock
18 artichoke hearts, halved
8 tablespoons (1 stick) unsalted butter
Chopped fresh parsley (garnish)

Sprinkle lamb generously with salt and pepper and oregano. Heat oil in large skillet over medium-high heat until haze forms. Add lamb in batches *(do not crowd)* and brown well on all sides, adding more oil as necessary. Transfer lamb to platter and keep warm. Add garlic to pan and sauté briefly. Pour off all but a thin film of oil. Add lemon juice to skillet and boil briskly over high heat, scraping up any browned bits clinging to bottom of pan. Stir in stock and artichokes. Continue cooking until sauce is reduced to a glaze. Return lamb to skillet, tossing gently to coat with sauce. Stir in butter 1 tablespoon at a time until sauce is desired consistency. Sprinkle mixture with parsley and toss gently. Transfer to heated platter and serve immediately.

🍃 *Béarnaise*

With the exception of hollandaise, béarnaise is the most prominent member of the warm emulsified sauce family—those made by beating butter into warm egg yolks to form a creamy emulsion. While hollandaise is flavored quite simply with lemon juice, which also aids in the binding of yolks and butter, béarnaise substitutes a more complex combination of vinegar, wine, tarragon and chervil, reduced to an aromatic essence called an infusion. The character of béarnaise provides the perfect balance for full-flavored meats such as grilled steak, veal chops and lamb chops.

Like hollandaise, béarnaise can be made with a whisk, a hand-held electric mixer, a food processor or a blender. No matter what means you use, there are two rules that must be observed: (1) warm the egg yolks very slowly and (2) add the butter very gradually.

Classic Sauce Béarnaise

Makes about 1 cup

1 teaspoon fresh tarragon *or* ½ teaspoon dried
1 teaspoon fresh chervil *or* ½ teaspoon dried

¼ cup tarragon vinegar *or* white wine vinegar
¼ cup dry white wine *or* dry vermouth
1 tablespoon minced shallot *or* green onion (white part only)
1 tablespoon fresh tarragon *or* 1½ teaspoons dried

1 tablespoon fresh chervil *or* 1½ teaspoons dried
Pinch *each* of salt and freshly ground pepper

4 egg yolks, beaten until creamy
1 tablespoon water
¾ cup (1½ sticks) unsalted butter, melted
1 teaspoon fresh lemon juice
Pinch of ground red pepper

Tie first 2 ingredients in 2 thicknesses of cheesecloth. Dip quickly into boiling water, then cold water; squeeze dry.* Discard cheesecloth; set herbs aside.

Mix next 5 ingredients with salt and pepper in small saucepan. Bring to boil, reduce heat and simmer until mixture is reduced to about 2 tablespoons. Cool slightly and strain into heavy-bottomed 1-quart nonaluminum saucepan,** pressing herbs with back of spoon to release the infusion.

Add egg yolks and water to vinegar-wine-herb infusion and mix thoroughly. Whisk (or beat with electric mixer set on medium speed) over low heat until thickened, about 3 to 4 minutes. Do not allow eggs to become too thick or dry. Remove from heat and begin slowly drizzling warm, not hot, melted butter into yolks, beating constantly until all butter has been added and sauce is thick and creamy. If it is too thick to pour, thin with a little hot water. Stir in the reserved steeped herbs, lemon juice and ground red pepper.

*This releases the flavors of the herbs and preserves (or renews, in the case of dried herbs) their naturally fresh green color.

**If heavy pan is not available, protect sauce from direct heat by standing pan on a heat diffuser; or make sauce in double boiler with 2 inches of very hot, but not simmering, water in bottom. In double boiler, eggs will require about 10 minutes of beating to reach the correct consistency.

Blender Sauce Béarnaise

Makes about 1½ cups

2 tablespoons tarragon vinegar *or* white wine vinegar
2 tablespoons dry white wine *or* dry vermouth
1½ tablespoons minced shallot *or* green onion (white part only)
2 teaspoons fresh tarragon *or* 1 teaspoon dried
4 egg yolks

¼ teaspoon salt
Pinch of freshly ground white pepper
⅛ teaspoon Glace de Viande (meat glaze) (optional), see page 11
1 cup (2 sticks) unsalted butter, melted and sizzling hot*

Combine first 4 ingredients in small saucepan and simmer until 1 tablespoon of liquid remains. Transfer to blender or processor and add yolks, salt, pepper and Glace de Viande, if desired. Blend until thoroughly mixed. With machine running, pour hot butter into egg mixture in a slow, steady stream (it should take about 15 seconds).

*Butter must be sizzling hot when it is added or sauce will not thicken properly.

Variations on Classic Béarnaise

Choron: Peel, seed and coarsely chop 1 large ripe tomato. Sauté briefly in 2 tablespoons butter over moderate heat. Stir in 1 tablespoon tomato paste and bring to a boil. Fold into béarnaise in place of steeped herbs. Serve with steaks, fish, chicken or poached eggs.

Foyot: Substitute 2 tablespoons Glace de Viande (meat glaze) for steeped tarragon and chervil. Serve with poached cubes of veal.

Paloise: Substitute equal quantity of fresh mint for tarragon. Serve with vegetables or broiled lamb chops.

Chivry: Substitute 1 to 2 teaspoons (depending on depth of color preferred) pureed watercress, spinach or parsley for steeped chervil and tarragon. Serve with grilled or sautéed meats.

Great Hints

• The herb infusion can be made in larger quantities and stored. Ingredients can be readily multiplied in any quantity desired. Store in tightly covered jar in refrigerator. Use 1 teaspoon strained infusion for each yolk.

• Béarnaise may be stored in a tightly closed, wide-necked vacuum bottle that has been preheated with hot water; emulsion will retain its smooth, stable consistency for several hours.

• To preserve fresh tarragon: Chop and place in a jar with tight-fitting lid. Add enough vinegar to cover.

Miniature Lamb Patties with Sauce Basquaise

The savory, vividly colored sauce is excellent with other meats, too.

Makes about 16 patties

Sauce Basquaise
- 3 tablespoons olive oil
- 2 large onions, coarsely chopped
- 2 red bell peppers, cored, seeded and diced
- 1 green bell pepper, cored, seeded and diced
- 4 ounces smoked ham, diced
- 4 garlic cloves, minced
- 2 tablespoons brandy
- 1 2-pound 3-ounce can tomatoes, drained and chopped
- ¼ cup dry white wine
- 1 teaspoon salt, or to taste
- ¼ teaspoon *each* dried thyme, oregano and basil
- ¼ cup chopped fresh parsley
- Freshly ground pepper

Lamb Patties
- 2 pounds ground lamb shoulder
- ⅓ cup pine nuts *or* chopped walnuts, lightly toasted (toast 10 minutes at 350°F)
- ¼ cup chopped fresh parsley
- 2 garlic cloves, minced
- 1 teaspoon salt
- ¼ teaspoon freshly ground pepper

- 3 tablespoons olive oil

- ½ cup dry white wine
- Chopped fresh parsley (garnish)

For sauce Basquaise: Heat 3 tablespoons olive oil in heavy large skillet over medium-low heat. Add onion and cook until soft, about 7 to 8 minutes. Stir in red and green bell peppers, cover and cook 5 minutes. Stir in ham and garlic and cook uncovered 4 minutes. Add brandy, scraping up any browned bits. Blend in tomato, ¼ cup wine, salt and dried herbs. Increase heat to medium high and cook, stirring frequently, until peppers are tender and sauce has thickened, about 10 minutes. *(Can be prepared up to 3 days ahead to this point, cooled, covered and refrigerated. Reheat before proceeding.)* Stir in parsley and pepper. Taste and adjust seasoning.

For lamb patties: Combine lamb, pine nuts, ¼ cup parsley, 1 teaspoon salt and ¼ teaspoon pepper in large bowl and mix lightly. Gently form into patties about ¾ inch thick and 2½ to 3 inches in diameter. Cover with plastic wrap and set aside. *(Patties can be prepared up to 1 day ahead.)*

Pat lamb patties dry. Heat 3 tablespoons olive oil in another large skillet over medium-high heat. Add patties (in batches if necessary; *do not crowd*) and sauté until seared on both sides and medium rare inside, about 4 minutes total. Arrange on heated platter and keep warm.

Pour off excess fat from skillet. Add ½ cup wine to skillet, increase heat to high and boil rapidly until reduced by half, scraping up any browned bits. Pour evenly over patties. Garnish with parsley. Reheat Sauce Basquaise if necessary. Serve immediately with lamb.

Lamb Chops Korabiak

4 servings

¼ cup (½ stick) butter
6 to 10 mushrooms, sliced
2 to 3 green onions, sliced
2 large *or* 4 small lamb chops
1 teaspoon minced fresh rosemary
  or ½ teaspoon dried

Garlic powder
Salt and freshly ground pepper
1 cup dry red wine

Melt half of butter in large skillet over medium-high heat. Add mushrooms and onions and sauté until tender, about 5 to 10 minutes. Remove and keep warm. Melt remaining butter in same skillet over medium-high heat. Sprinkle chops with rosemary, garlic powder and salt and pepper. Add to skillet and sauté until browned on both sides, about 5 minutes. Reduce heat to medium and continue cooking until tender. Transfer lamb chops to heated platter. Pour wine into skillet and cook over medium-high heat, scraping up any browned bits clinging to bottom of pan, until liquid is reduced by about ⅓. Spoon vegetables over chops and top with sauce.

Mustard-Ginger Lamb Chops
with Vegetable Garnish

4 servings

4 garlic cloves, crushed
1 2-inch piece ginger, peeled and
  coarsely chopped
2 teaspoons dry vermouth
2 teaspoons fresh lime juice
2 teaspoons white wine thyme
  vinegar*
¼ teaspoon crushed red peppercorns
¼ teaspoon crushed green
  peppercorns
  Pinch of salt
1 cup (scant) extra-strong Dijon
  mustard
1 teaspoon unrefined orange
  blossom honey

Salt and freshly ground pepper
16 New Zealand lamb chops *or* 8
  small American chops, trimmed
  of all fat and gristle, frenched
6 to 8 slices whole wheat bread,
  toasted, mixed in blender and
  sieved

8 tablespoons (1 stick) butter,
  melted and clarified
⅓ cup chopped fresh parsley
⅓ cup chopped shallot

Combine garlic, ginger, vermouth, lime juice, thyme vinegar, peppercorns and salt in small saucepan and cook over medium-high heat until reduced by half. Add mustard and honey and bring to boil, stirring constantly, until slightly reduced, about 5 to 8 minutes (mixture will be sticky). Strain through cheesecloth into jar with tight-fitting lid and seal tightly. Refrigerate until ready to use. *(Can be prepared up to 6 weeks ahead.)*

Lightly sprinkle salt and pepper over both sides of lamb chops. Spread 1½ to 2 teaspoons mustard mixture over all sides of each chop (if using American lamb, increase mustard to 2 to 3 teaspoons per chop). Dip all sides into breadcrumbs, covering completely and patting gently so breadcrumbs adhere.

Heat 4 tablespoons butter in large skillet over medium-high heat until foam subsides. Add half of chops and brown on both sides (*be careful not to burn; chops should be medium rare*). Transfer to platter and keep warm. Repeat with remaining chops. Blend parsley and shallot, sprinkle lightly over top of each lamb chop and serve.

*For white wine thyme vinegar, combine ¼ cup white wine vinegar and 1 teaspoon dried thyme in small saucepan and bring to simmer over medium heat; simmer 5 minutes. Strain well before using.

Sliced Lamb with Hot Spice (Shaptak)

This recipe can be doubled easily.

2 servings

2 tablespoons corn *or* peanut oil
¼ cup finely chopped onion
2 tablespoons minced garlic
2 tablespoons minced fresh ginger
½ teaspoon five-spice powder
¼ teaspoon salt
¾ pound lamb from leg *or* chop, sliced into thin 2-inch strips

1½ 5-inch fresh green chilies, seeded and sliced into ½-inch pieces
2 tablespoons hot water
2 tablespoons light soy sauce
1 teaspoon sugar

Heat oil in wok or heavy medium skillet over high heat. Add onion, garlic, ginger, five-spice powder and salt and stir 3 minutes. Add lamb and stir 1 minute. Blend in chilies, hot water, soy sauce and sugar and stir about 1 minute (or until lamb reaches desired doneness). Serve immediately.

Kan's Lamb

4 servings

¼ cup hoisin sauce*
2 tablespoons soy sauce
2 tablespoons sugar
2 tablespoons cornstarch
2 tablespoons vegetable oil
2 small garlic cloves, minced
2 teaspoons sesame oil*
2 teaspoons rice wine *or* Sherry
⅛ teaspoon freshly ground white pepper

2 pounds lean lamb, cut into 1½ × ⅛-inch cubes

¼ cup vegetable oil
2 tablespoons dark soy sauce
2 teaspoons sugar
Freshly cooked rice sticks (mai fun)* *or* rice

Combine first 9 ingredients in large bowl. Add lamb and mix well. Cover with plastic and refrigerate overnight.

Heat oil over high heat until very hot. Drain lamb well. Add to wok in batches and stir-fry until brown on all sides. Add 2 tablespoons dark soy sauce and 2 teaspoons sugar and stir-fry for 30 seconds. Transfer to platter. Serve hot over rice sticks or rice.

*Available in oriental markets.

Chinese One-dish Lamb

If using rice sticks, deep fry in oil until just puffed and drain well.

2 to 3 servings

2 teaspoons hoisin sauce*
1 teaspoon oyster sauce
1 teaspoon plum sauce*
½ teaspoon soy sauce
½ teaspoon tomato paste
½ teaspoon cornstarch
¼ teaspoon salt
¼ teaspoon sugar

2 teaspoons cornstarch
⅔ pound boned lamb, sliced ⅛ inch thick

2 tablespoon vegetable oil
½ cup shredded bok choy (Chinese cabbage) *or* thinly sliced celery
¼ cup shredded carrot
¼ cup sliced bamboo shoots
3 green onions, thinly sliced
½ teaspoon salt
½ teaspoon sugar
Freshly cooked rice *or* deep-fried rice sticks (mai fun)*

Mix first 8 ingredients in small bowl and set aside.
Rub cornstarch into meat in bowl.
Heat wok or skillet over high heat. Add 1 tablespoon oil and swirl to coat. Add bok choy, carrot, bamboo shoots, onions, salt and sugar and stir-fry until vegetables are crisp-tender, about 3 minutes. Transfer to platter. Add remaining oil to wok. Add lamb and stir-fry about 2 minutes. Blend in reserved sauce and continue to cook about 1 minute. Reduce heat to medium, return vegetables to wok and stir-fry until heated through, about 2 minutes. Serve over cooked rice or rice sticks.

*Available in oriental markets.

❧ Roasting and Baking

Stuffed Leg of Lamb Wrapped in Pastry (Bouty Arniou Ghemisto Zimaropeplomeno)

6 to 8 servings

Stuffing
¾ pound lean ground pork
3 green onions, chopped
1 egg, lightly beaten
½ cup chopped fresh parsley
1 tablespoon minced orange peel
¾ teaspoon ground cumin
½ teaspoon freshly ground pepper
Salt

Pastry
2 tablespoons sugar
1½ tablespoons active dry yeast
½ cup warm water (105°F to 115°F)
6 cups all purpose flour
1 teaspoon salt
½ cup (1 stick) butter, diced

1½ cups milk, room temperature

Lamb
1 5- to 6-pound leg of lamb, boned and trimmed
3 tablespoons butter, room temperature
2 to 3 large garlic cloves, crushed
1 teaspoon salt
¾ teaspoon freshly ground pepper
1 tablespoon fresh rosemary, crushed

1 egg yolk
1 tablespoon milk

Fresh mint leaves (garnish)

For stuffing: Combine all ingredients and blend well. Cover and refrigerate.

For pastry: Dissolve sugar and yeast in water and let stand until foamy and proofed. Combine flour and 1 teaspoon salt in large bowl. Using your hands, rub diced butter into flour until it is absorbed. Make well in center of flour and pour in yeast and milk. Still using hands, push flour from sides of bowl into center and mix to form dough. Knead several minutes until smooth. Place in lightly oiled bowl and turn to coat. Cover with plastic wrap and let rise in warm area until doubled in size, about 1 hour.

For lamb: Preheat oven to 450°F. Set butterflied lamb, skin side down, on working surface. Pound to flatten slightly. Mix 3 tablespoons butter, garlic, 1 teaspoon salt and ¾ teaspoon pepper to a paste. Rub half thoroughly into lamb. Spread with stuffing and reshape leg. Sew closed with kitchen string; tie crosswise at 1-inch intervals and twice around length to hold stuffing. Rub outside with remaining butter mixture, then rub with rosemary. Set on rack in roasting pan and roast 20 minutes. Reduce oven temperature to 350°F and roast an additional 40 minutes. Let cool, then remove string and brush off excess rosemary.

Lightly oil shallow roasting pan. Knead dough once again. Roll out enough dough on lightly floured surface to make rectangle ¼ inch thick, large enough to enclose lamb completely with 1-inch overlap. Set lamb on one end of rectangle. Beat yolk with milk and brush some on edges of dough. Fold dough over lamb. Press seams together; trim and reserve excess dough. Set seam side down in roasting pan and brush with some of yolk.

Preheat oven to 450°F. Roll excess dough into long thin ropes. Make braid long enough to go around top perimeter of lamb. Brush with yolk mixture. Bake until pastry sets, about 15 minutes. Reduce oven temperature to 300°F and bake until meat thermometer inserted in thickest portion registers desired degree of doneness, about 130°F for medium rare (about 20 to 30 minutes more). Transfer to heated serving platter and garnish with mint leaves. Let lamb stand several minutes before slicing.

Lamb Chieti Style (Agnello alla Chietina)

Chieti is a city of the Abruzzi near the Adriatic Sea, and cooks there have created a unique roast: The long, protruding portion of bone is usually cut off a leg of lamb, but in this recipe—for easier handling and a more dramatic presentation—it is left on. Potatoes are an excellent accompaniment.

6 to 8 servings

3 tablespoons coarsely chopped prosciutto fat *or* bacon
2 parsley sprigs, minced
1 large garlic clove, minced
1 tablespoon fresh rosemary leaves *or* 1 teaspoon dried
1 5-pound leg of lamb, patted dry

¼ cup olive oil
Salt and freshly ground pepper
¼ cup red wine vinegar

¾ cup very fine dry breadcrumbs
½ cup minced fresh parsley
1 tablespoon minced fresh mint

Preheat oven to 400°F. Combine prosciutto fat, minced parsley sprigs, garlic and rosemary; freeze briefly to facilitate handling. Make several long thin holes in lamb with sharp knife. Widen and lengthen holes slightly by piercing with handle of wooden spoon. Pack parsley mixture into each hole.

Pour oil into roasting pan. Roll lamb in oil so meat is evenly coated. Sprinkle with pepper. Roast 15 minutes. Reduce oven temperature to 350°F and continue roasting until thermometer registers 125°F, sprinkling meat with salt once and basting with vinegar several times, about 50 minutes for rare. Set aside. Maintain oven temperature.

Combine breadcrumbs, ½ cup parsley and mint and baking sheet. Hold lamb bone using kitchen towel or pot holder and roll lamb evenly in breadcrumb mixture. Return to roasting pan. Baste with pan juices. Continue roasting until coating is brown, 15 to 20 minutes. Cool 15 minutes before carving.

Butterflied Leg of Lamb with Parmesan Crust

8 to 10 servings

¼ cup olive oil
2 teaspoons minced garlic
1 teaspoon dried tarragon
1 7-pound leg of lamb, boned and butterflied

¼ cup Dijon mustard
½ cup freshly grated Parmesan cheese

3 tablespoons minced fresh parsley
2 tablespoons fine dry breadcrumbs
2 tablespoons (¼ stick) unsalted butter, melted
Fresh mint *or* parsley sprigs

Blend oil with garlic and tarragon in small bowl. Brush over lamb. Let stand at room temperature 2 hours.

Preheat broiler. Place meat, fat side down, in shallow baking pan. Brush with half of mustard. Broil 6 inches from heat source 5 minutes. Turn meat, brush with remaining mustard and broil 5 minutes. Turn oven temperature to 450°F. Blend cheese, minced parsley and breadcrumbs in small bowl. Sprinkle over meat, patting gently so crumbs adhere. Drizzle with melted butter. Roast until crumbs are crisp and brown and thermometer inserted in thickest portion of meat registers desired degree of doneness, about 130°F for rare. Let stand about 10 minutes before carving. Garnish with fresh mint sprigs.

Turban of Lamb with Apricot–Wild Rice Stuffing

This presentation is spectacular. The wild rice, nut and apricot stuffing complements the meat perfectly.

8 servings

Wild Rice Stuffing
½ cup diced dried apricots

3 tablespoons unsalted butter
2 medium onions, chopped
2 cups wild rice, rinsed and drained
5 cups chicken stock
½ cup chopped almonds, toasted (toast 10 minutes at 350°F)
¼ cup minced fresh parsley
Salt and freshly ground pepper

1 7-pound leg of lamb, boned, butterflied and trimmed

2 tablespoons Cognac

Glaze
¼ cup Dijon mustard
2 tablespoons vegetable oil
2 medium garlic cloves, minced
1 teaspoon dried rosemary
¼ teaspoon freshly ground pepper

Steamed broccoli florets
Cherry tomatoes

For wild rice stuffing: Soak apricots in water to cover 2½ hours, turning occasionally.

Melt butter in heavy large saucepan over medium-low heat. Add onions, cover and cook until translucent, stirring occasionally, about 10 minutes. Mix in wild rice to coat with butter. Add stock, drained apricots, almonds and parsley. Bring to boil. Reduce heat, cover and simmer until rice is tender and slightly puffed, about 50 minutes. Season with salt and pepper.

Place lamb on work surface, fat side down. Score if necessary to open out flat. Sprinkle with Cognac and salt and pepper. Pat ½-inch layer of stuffing over meat and into score marks, leaving 1-inch border. Spoon remaining stuffing into buttered 2-quart baking dish; cover with buttered parchment paper. Thread trussing needle with 3 feet of kitchen twine. Stitch loosely around circumference of lamb. Pull ends of twine to gather lamb into ball; tie securely. Wrap ends of twine around ball to secure shape.

For glaze: Combine mustard, oil, garlic, rosemary and pepper in small bowl. Oil rack and set in roasting pan. Place pan in center of oven and preheat to

425°F. Pat lamb dry, then rub glaze over. Place lamb, seam side down, on rack. Roast 20 minutes. Reduce oven temperature to 375°F. Continue cooking until thermometer inserted in thickest portion of meat registers desired degree of doneness, about 130°F for medium rare (about 1½ hours). Bake rice stuffing in dish during last 30 minutes of roasting time.

Let lamb rest 10 minutes. Discard string. Place lamb on round serving platter and surround with broccoli and tomatoes. Cut lamb into wedges. Serve additional stuffing alongside.

Yorkshire Deviled Shoulder of Lamb

Accompany each serving with a bit of the savory deviled crust and some sausage stuffing. Offer a tart plum, quince or red currant jam alongside.

6 to 8 servings

Sausage Stuffing
- 1 pound bulk sausage
- 2 tablespoons (¼ stick) butter
- ½ cup minced onion
- ⅓ cup chopped mixed fresh herbs (such as parsley, thyme and mint)
- 1 teaspoon dried sage
- 1 cup fresh breadcrumbs
- ⅓ cup dry Sherry
- 1 egg, lightly beaten
  Grated peel of 1 lemon
  Salt and freshly ground pepper

- 1 4- to 5-pound lamb shoulder, boned,* room temperature
- ½ lemon
- 2 tablespoons seasoning flour,** or more

Deviled Crust
- ½ cup fresh breadcrumbs
- 3 tablespoons English *or* Dijon mustard
- 1 tablespoon vegetable oil
- 1 teaspoon paprika
- ½ teaspoon mace
- ½ teaspoon freshly grated nutmeg
- ½ teaspoon salt
- ¼ teaspoon ground red pepper
- 1 garlic clove, pressed
  Juice and grated peel of 1 medium lemon

Fresh watercress sprigs (garnish)
Additional dry Sherry (optional)
Lamb *or* beef stock (optional)

For sausage stuffing: Cook sausage in nonstick large skillet over medium heat until fat is rendered, 5 to 6 minutes. Discard fat. Transfer sausage to large bowl. Melt butter in same skillet over low heat. Stir in onion, cover and cook until translucent, about 10 minutes. Remove from heat. Add fresh herbs and sage to onion and toss gently to blend. Add breadcrumbs, Sherry, egg, lemon peel, salt and pepper and onion mixture to sausage and blend well; mixture should hold together. Let cool.

Preheat oven to 350°F. Spread stuffing evenly over boned lamb. Roll into log shape, fat side out, and tie with string at 2-inch intervals. Rub entire surface with cut side of lemon. Sprinkle evenly with seasoning flour, using enough to cover entire surface. Transfer lamb to parchment paper–lined roasting pan. Roast uncovered 1 hour.

For deviled crust: Mix all ingredients in small bowl and set aside.

Remove lamb from oven and coat entire surface with crust mixture. Return to oven and continue roasting until crust is golden and lamb is tender, pink and juicy, about 1 hour. Transfer to heated platter. Let stand 10 to 15 minutes before cutting into thick slices. Garnish each serving with watercress sprigs. Deglaze pan juices with additional Sherry and stock. Reduce juices to saucelike consistency and serve.

*Lamb shoulder with bone in can be substituted. Make long slashes across surface of meat, spacing cuts about 1 inch apart. Rub with lemon, then sprinkle with seasoning flour. Cut pocket large enough to contain stuffing under fatty surface. Continue as described in recipe instructions.

**For seasoning flour, combine 2 tablespoons all purpose flour, 1 teaspoon salt and ½ teaspoon freshly ground pepper in small cup. Makes about 2½ tablespoons.

Roast Saddle of Lamb with Herbs and Green Onions

At L'Ermitage in Los Angeles, this is occasionally served with a julienne of eggplant flavored with fresh basil and tarragon and topped with chopped tomato.

4 servings

Sauce
- 2 to 3 tablespoons unsalted butter
- ½ pound lamb bones and trimmings
- 1 medium onion, chopped
- 1 medium carrot, chopped
- 1 medium celery stalk, chopped
- 1 garlic clove, halved
- 4 cups chicken stock
- 4 cups veal stock
- 2 tablespoons dry white wine
- 2 bay leaves
- 2 fresh thyme sprigs, chopped, *or* ½ teaspoon dried
- 2 fresh parsley sprigs, chopped
- ½ teaspoon dried tarragon
- 4 to 5 fresh basil leaves, chopped, *or* ½ teaspoon dried

Spinach Mousseline
- ½ bunch fresh spinach, stemmed (about 3 ounces)
- ¼ pound lean ground veal
- 1 egg white
- 1½ teaspoons salt
- ¾ teaspoon freshly ground white pepper
- 2 tablespoons (¼ stick) unsalted butter, room temperature
- 1 cup whipping cream

- 2 tablespoons clarified unsalted butter
- 1 2-pound lamb loin, boned and trimmed

- 1 piece caul fat* (about 5 × 10 inches)

- 15 green onions (white part only), blanched in 2 cups water and 2 tablespoons butter

For sauce: Melt 2 to 3 tablespoons butter in large skillet over high heat. Add lamb bones and trimmings and sauté until browned, about 2 minutes. Stir in onion, carrot, celery and garlic and sauté until browned. Pour off fat and discard. Blend next 8 ingredients. Reduce heat to low and simmer gently 2 hours. Strain sauce; return liquid to skillet. Continue cooking until reduced to approximately 4½ cups. Set aside.

For spinach mousseline: Bring 6 to 8 cups salted water to rapid boil in large saucepan. Add spinach and stir 5 seconds. Immediately drain and rinse under cold water. Drain well; pat dry with paper towel. Chop spinach into ½-inch dice. Refrigerate until ready to use.

Combine ground veal, egg white and salt and pepper in processor and mix until very smooth, 2 to 3 minutes, stopping several times to scrape down sides of work bowl. Add 2 tablespoons butter and mix 2 minutes. With machine running, slowly add cream, mixing until completely smooth, 3 to 4 minutes. Transfer mousseline to large bowl. Gently fold in spinach. Cover and refrigerate until ready to use.

Heat 2 tablespoons clarified butter in large skillet over high heat. Add lamb and sauté just until well browned on all sides, about 5 minutes. Let lamb cool to room temperature.

Preheat oven to 450°F. Lightly butter shallow baking dish large enough to contain lamb. Unfold caul fat on work surface. Spread half of mousseline over caul fat in area about size of lamb. Set lamb over mousseline. Top lamb with remaining mousseline, then spread some down sides to enclose lamb completely. Bring sides of caul fat up around lamb, twisting ends to seal. Press gently to distribute mousseline evenly. Transfer lamb to prepared baking dish. Roast to desired doneness, about 25 minutes for medium rare.

To serve, gently reheat sauce. Cut lamb into even number of ½- to ¾-inch slices. Arrange slices in circular pattern on individual plates, dividing evenly. Tuck green onion between each slice. Remove bay leaves and spoon sauce over top.

*Available in specialty butcher shops.

Crown Roast of Lamb

Ringed with meatballs, glazed apples and a wreath of laurel leaves, this roast makes a hearty yet elegant meal.

8 servings

Fresh lemon juice
1 7- to 8-pound crown roast of lamb, trimmed of all fat
Salt and freshly ground pepper

½ cup Dijon mustard
2 tablespoons soy sauce
2 garlic cloves, minced
1 teaspoon dried rosemary

¼ teaspoon ground marjoram

Freshly cooked wild rice
Lamb Meatballs (see following recipes)
Glazed May Apples (see following recipes)
Wreath of laurel leaves (optional decoration)

Preheat oven to 325°F. Moisten paper towel with lemon juice and rub over lamb. Insert meat thermometer into meatiest section of roast, being careful not to touch bone. Place on rack in roasting pan and sprinkle with salt and pepper to taste. Cover tips of bones with foil to prevent burning; crumple additional foil and place in center of roast to help retain shape. Roast until thermometer registers 120°F.

Meanwhile, combine next 5 ingredients in small bowl and blend well. When 120°F temperature is reached, discard foil from center of roast and paint inside of meat generously with mustard mixture. Continue roasting until thermometer registers desired degree of doneness, about 135°F for medium rare.

To serve, fill center of lamb with wild rice. Ring meatballs around outside and surround with glazed apples. Decorate with wreath of laurel leaves.

Lamb Meatballs

Makes about 45 meatballs

2 tablespoons (¼ stick) unsalted butter
5 shallots, minced
2 pounds ground lamb
1 cup fresh breadcrumbs
¼ cup chopped fresh parsley
1 egg, lightly beaten

2 tablespoons finely grated lemon peel
½ teaspoon ground marjoram
Salt and freshly ground pepper

1 tablespoon unsalted butter
1 tablespoon olive oil

Melt 2 tablespoons butter in small skillet over medium heat. Add shallots and sauté until softened. Transfer to large bowl and add lamb, breadcrumbs, parsley, egg, lemon peel, marjoram and salt and pepper and blend well. Form into balls about the size of chestnuts.

Heat remaining butter with oil in large skillet over medium-high heat. Add meatballs in batches and sauté until browned on all sides and cooked as desired. Drain on paper towels. Reheat in low oven before serving.

Glazed May Apples

8 servings

16 May apples *or* other small baking apples, peeled but not cored
2 tablespoons sugar, or to taste
1½ cups apple cider

1 cup currant jelly, melted
Red food coloring

Preheat oven to 300°F. Arrange apples in large, shallow baking dish and dust with sugar. Pour in cider. Bake, basting several times, until apples are tender when pierced with fork but still hold their shape, 30 to 45 minutes.

Transfer apples to shallow serving platter. Add jelly to juices in baking dish and blend well. Tint with food coloring. Pour over apples to glaze. Let cool, then refrigerate. Serve chilled.

Barbecued Saddle of Lamb

This recipe can be adapted for a smaller leg of lamb (bone in). Adjust the ingredient amounts accordingly, and cook as described, or in a 450°F oven. Roast 15 minutes, then reduce oven temperature to 350°F and continue roasting 10 minutes per pound for medium rare.

24 servings

1 22-pound saddle of lamb
10 large garlic cloves, slivered
½ cup olive oil (preferably Greek), or more
½ cup fresh lemon juice, or more
¼ cup minced fresh oregano, or more
Salt and freshly ground pepper

Prepare barbecue grill with rotisserie attachment. Secure lamb on rotisserie skewer. Insert garlic slivers in meaty part of lamb and under skin; *do not pierce skin.* Gradually whisk olive oil into lemon juice. Brush meat generously with some of mixture. Combine oregano and salt and pepper. Rub mixture into meat. Sprinkle with additional oregano if desired. Roast lamb until meat thermometer inserted in thickest portion of meat registers desired degree of doneness, about 130°F for medium rare (about 3 hours), basting with remaining oil and juice every 20 minutes. Add more olive oil and lemon juice if necessary. Let lamb stand 15 minutes before carving.

Rack of Lamb Moutarde

6 servings

Veal and Tomato Sauce
2½ pounds veal bones, cut up

1 large onion, sliced
2 carrots, sliced
1 garlic clove
Bouquet garni (thyme, parsley and bay leaf, tied together in a cheesecloth bag)

2 tablespoons peanut oil
1 small carrot, finely chopped
1 small onion, finely chopped
3 fresh tomatoes, chopped
1½ teaspoons tomato paste

1 celery stalk, cut up
Parsley sprigs
5 peppercorns, lightly crushed

Lamb
2 racks of lamb, all fat removed
¼ cup Dijon mustard
1½ teaspoons light soy sauce
1½ teaspoons dark soy sauce
1 garlic clove, minced
½ teaspoon ground sage
½ teaspoon dried marjoram
⅛ teaspoon ground ginger

For veal and tomato sauce: Preheat oven to 475°F. Spread bones on large baking sheet. Roast, turning once or twice until well browned, about 45 minutes.

Combine bones, sliced onion, sliced carrots, garlic and bouquet garni in large stockpot with enough water to cover. Place over high heat and bring to vigorous boil. Reduce heat and boil gently about 4 hours, skimming foam from surface.

Strain stock through fine sieve set over large bowl (you should have about 2 cups of brown veal stock). Let stock cool. Remove and discard any fat from surface. Set stock aside. *(Stock can be prepared ahead and refrigerated or frozen. Reheat when ready to use.)*

Heat oil in medium saucepan over medium heat. Add chopped carrot and chopped onion and sauté until golden. Reduce heat to low. Add remaining ingredients with cooled veal stock and simmer until reduced by half. Strain through fine sieve into small mixing bowl, pressing vegetables with back of spoon to extract as much liquid as possible. Keep warm.

For lamb: Preheat oven to 400°F. Arrange lamb racks on baking sheet, bone side down. Combine remaining ingredients in small bowl, blending well. Coat meat thoroughly with mixture. Roast lamb until tender, about 15 to 20 minutes. Transfer racks to platter and serve. Serve sauce separately.

Rack of Lamb Battuto

In Italy meat is often flavored with battuto—a mixture of oil, seasonings and lemon juice or vinegar. The ingredients are worked into a paste that is spread over the meat as long as 24 hours before cooking.

2 servings

4 juniper berries
1 garlic clove, minced
½ teaspoon grated lemon peel
¼ teaspoon freshly ground pepper

2 tablespoons olive oil
1 teaspoon fresh lemon juice
1 4-rib rack of lamb, trimmed*

Combine juniper berries, garlic, lemon peel and pepper in mortar and work with pestle until mixture is smooth. Gradually add oil drop by drop, mixing constantly until thoroughly blended. Slowly blend in lemon juice. Spread mixture over lamb. Wrap meat loosely in waxed paper and refrigerate for at least 8 hours, or up to 24 hours.

Preheat oven to 475°F. Roast lamb, meaty side down, for 10 minutes. Turn lamb over, reduce oven temperature to 400°F and continue roasting until meat thermometer registers desired degree of doneness, about 125° for rare, 140°F for medium and 150° to 160°F for well done.

*If your butcher won't sell you a 4-rib rack of lamb, buy one of the conventional 8-rib racks and cut it in half, freezing the remainder for a later meal. Be sure the butcher cracks the chine between the ribs for easier carving.

Lamb Pastitsio

A very hearty layered casserole.

2 servings

1 tablespoon olive oil
½ small onion, finely chopped
2 garlic cloves, minced
½ pound lean ground lamb
¾ cup tomato sauce
2 tablespoons minced fresh parsley
¼ teaspoon dried rosemary
Pinch of cinnamon
Salt and freshly ground pepper

2 tablespoons (¼ stick) butter
1 teaspoon all purpose flour

¾ cup milk
2 tablespoons freshly grated Parmesan cheese
Pinch of freshly grated nutmeg

¼ pound ziti *or* other macaroni-type pasta
1 egg, beaten to blend

½ cup grated Swiss cheese
Freshly grated nutmeg

Heat oil in heavy medium skillet over medium heat. Add onion and garlic and stir until soft, about 5 minutes. Add lamb and stir until almost cooked, with some pink remaining. Drain off fat. Blend in tomato sauce, parsley, rosemary and cinnamon. Season with salt and pepper. Set aside.

Melt 1 tablespoon butter in heavy small saucepan over medium-low heat. Blend in flour with wooden spoon and stir 3 minutes. Gradually add milk, whisking until sauce thickens and just comes to boil, about 5 minutes. Remove sauce from heat. Stir in Parmesan and nutmeg. Set aside.

Preheat oven to 375°F. Cook pasta in large pot of boiling salted water until al dente, about 10 minutes. Drain well and return to pot. Mix in egg and remaining 1 tablespoon butter.

Grease 2 small gratin or baking dishes. Divide half of pasta between dishes. Cover with all of lamb. Sprinkle each with half of cheese. Top with remaining pasta. Spoon sauce over and sprinkle with remaining cheese. Dust lightly with nutmeg. *(Can be prepared 2 days ahead to this point. Cover and refrigerate. Bring to room temperature before baking.)* Bake until tops are puffy and golden, 55 to 60 minutes. Serve hot.

Loin of Lamb Beauharnais

2 servings

1 1½-pound lamb loin, boned and cut into four 2-ounce medallions about 1½ inches in diameter
Salt and freshly ground pepper
¼ cup clarified butter

1 17¼-ounce package frozen puff pastry, thawed

6 tablespoons unsweetened chestnut puree
1 egg beaten with 1 teaspoon water
Madeira Sauce (see following recipe)

Pat meat dry. Season with salt and pepper. Heat butter in heavy large skillet over medium heat until hot but not smoking. Add medallions and sear 1 minute on each side. Set aside.

Preheat oven to 450°F. Cut 4 pastry rectangles about 1 inch wide and long enough to wrap around medallions; ¼ inch of meat will show at each end. (Remaining pastry can be frozen for another use.) Spread 1½ tablespoons chestnut puree over each rectangle, leaving ¼-inch borders at top ends. Set medallions with grain of meat running crosswise at bottom of each rectangle. Brush top ends with egg glaze. Beginning at bottom of each rectangle, roll up as for jelly roll. Brush pastry casings evenly with egg glaze. Arrange seam side down in small baking pan. Bake until pastry is puffed and golden brown and lamb is medium rare, about 10 minutes. Arrange 2 lamb packages on each plate. Spoon some of Madeira Sauce around each and serve. Serve remaining sauce separately.

Madeira Sauce

Makes 1 cup

2 tablespoons (¼ stick) unsalted butter
1 teaspoon minced shallot
½ cup sliced mushrooms

¾ cup Madeira
1 cup whipping cream
Salt and freshly ground pepper

Melt butter in heavy medium saucepan over medium heat. Add shallot and stir until limp, about 5 minutes. Add mushrooms and stir until almost all liquid evaporates, about 5 minutes. Blend in Madeira and boil until liquid is reduced to ¼ cup, stirring occasionally, about 15 minutes. Add cream and boil until sauce thickens. Season with salt and pepper. Use immediately.

Greek Lamb Terrine

Prepare at least 1 day ahead.

6 servings

3 tablespoons olive oil
1 pound fresh spinach, stemmed
Salt and freshly ground pepper

2 tablespoons (¼ stick) butter
1½ cups chopped onion
2 garlic cloves, minced
2 tablespoons all purpose flour
1 egg, beaten
2 pounds ground lamb
½ cup pistachios, shelled
¼ cup dry red wine

¼ cup minced fresh parsley
2 tablespoons minced fresh rosemary *or* 2 teaspoons dried
1 tablespoon grated orange peel
1 tablespoon fresh basil *or* 1 teaspoon dried
1 tablespoon salt
1 teaspoon coarsely ground pepper

3 slices bacon, halved crosswise and blanched 5 minutes

Heat olive oil in large skillet over medium-high heat. Gradually stir in spinach and sauté just until wilted. Season to taste with salt and pepper. Transfer to colander and let cool.

Preheat oven to 350°F. Melt butter in large skillet over low heat. Add onion and garlic. Cover and cook until onion is translucent, about 10 minutes, stirring occasionally. Set aside. Whisk flour and egg in large bowl. Add lamb, pistachios, wine, parsley, rosemary, orange peel, basil and salt and pepper. Add onion and mix thoroughly.

Pack half of meat mixture into bottom of 9¼ × 5¼ × 2¾-inch loaf pan. Squeeze spinach dry. Chop coarsely. Arrange spinach over top of meat, smoothing to form even layer. Add remaining meat mixture. Arrange bacon slices crosswise over top. Cover pan with aluminum foil. Set loaf pan into larger pan. Fill larger pan with enough boiling water to come halfway up sides of loaf pan. Bake terrine for 1½ hours.

Cool terrine 1 hour. Arrange foil-covered board or matching loaf pan over terrine and weight with several heavy cans. Refrigerate for 1 to 2 days. Remove bacon before serving.

Rosette of Lamb

6 servings

6 tablespoons (¾ stick) butter
6 5- to 6-ounce lamb fillets, cut from rack *or* loin

6 phyllo sheets (17 × 13 inches)
 Melted butter (for phyllo)
 Breadcrumbs
18 large spinach leaves, blanched, thoroughly drained and patted dry
 Salt and freshly ground pepper

3 medium carrots, cut julienne, blanched and patted dry

6 tablespoons finely chopped onion
1 garlic clove, crushed
 Pinch of dried rosemary
2 tablespoons fresh lemon juice
3 cups beef stock
2 tablespoons (¼ stick) butter, room temperature

Melt butter in medium skillet over medium-high heat until foam subsides. Add half of fillets and sauté quickly on all sides until browned. Remove lamb to platter and let cool slightly. Repeat with remaining fillets. Set skillet aside.

Preheat oven to 400°F. For each fillet, place sheet of phyllo on work surface (keep remainder covered with damp towel to prevent drying). Brush with melted butter. Fold in half crosswise and brush again with butter. Sprinkle with breadcrumbs. Lay 3 spinach leaves at one end of dough. Pat fillet dry with paper towel; reserve juices. Sprinkle meat with salt and pepper and set on spinach leaves. Top with carrots. Fold in sides of phyllo, then roll up and place seam side down on oiled baking sheet. Brush with butter and bake just until lightly browned, about 15 minutes.

Meanwhile, prepare sauce. Return skillet to medium-high heat. Add onion and sauté briefly. Stir in garlic and rosemary. Deglaze pan by adding lemon juice, reserved meat juices and stock. Season to taste with salt and pepper. Boil until reduced by ⅓. Remove from heat and stir in remaining butter. Serve lamb on heated plates and serve sauce separately.

Lamb Tart Avgolemono

You might precede this tart with artichokes served with Dijon mustard–flavored butter for dipping. Serve a salad of sliced beets and paper-thin slices of onion dressed with olive oil and cider vinegar lightly touched with ground cloves. A full dry red wine such as Barbera is a good choice.

6 to 8 servings

1 unbaked 9-inch pie shell
1 egg white, lightly beaten

1 pound ground lamb
2 slices homemade-style white bread, crusts trimmed, torn into pieces
¼ cup milk
¼ cup minced fresh parsley
1 large onion, minced
1 large garlic clove, minced
1 teaspoon minced fresh mint leaves *or* ½ teaspoon dried
1 teaspoon salt
½ teaspoon freshly ground pepper
¼ teaspoon allspice
3 eggs
½ cup chicken stock
¼ cup whipping cream
2 tablespoons fresh lemon juice
2 teaspoons grated lemon peel

Preheat oven to 400°F. Brush pastry with egg white and bake 5 minutes. Let cool while preparing filling.

Combine next 10 ingredients in large bowl and mix gently but thoroughly. Spoon into prepared shell. Beat eggs lightly. Add remaining ingredients and mix well. Pour into shell and bake 15 minutes. Reduce oven temperature to 350°F and continue baking until custard is firm, about 15 more minutes. Let stand 5 minutes before slicing.

Lamb and Sausage Pie

6 to 8 servings

1 tablespoon butter
2 medium lamb shoulder chops, boned and cut into small pieces
2 hot Italian sausages
2 carrots, chopped
2 medium onions, chopped
¾ cup chopped fresh parsley
½ cup shredded red cabbage
3 tablespoons instant flour
1½ cups water
1 cup white wine
1 teaspoon salt
½ teaspoon freshly ground pepper
½ teaspoon dried thyme

Pâte Brisée
1 cup all purpose flour
¼ cup (½ stick) butter, cut into 4 pieces, well chilled
⅛ teaspoon salt
1 egg
1½ teaspoons fresh lemon juice

Melt 1 tablespoon butter in large skillet over medium heat. Add lamb and sausages and brown on all sides. Remove from heat and let cool. Remove sausages from skillet and cut into small pieces. Return to skillet. Stir in carrots, onions, parsley and cabbage. Return to medium heat and cook, stirring constantly, 3 to 4 minutes. Add instant flour and stir to coat meat and vegetables evenly. Add water, wine, 1 teaspoon salt, pepper and thyme and stir through. Increase heat to high and bring mixture to boil. Reduce heat and simmer until lamb is cooked, about 45 minutes.

For pâte brisée: Combine flour, ¼ cup butter and ⅛ teaspoon salt in processor and blend using on/off turns until mixture resembles coarse meal; *do not overmix.* Add egg and lemon juice and mix just until ball forms. (Dough can also be prepared in medium bowl with pastry blender or 2 knives.) Cover dough with plastic wrap and refrigerate 1 hour before using.

Preheat oven to 375°F. Transfer stew to shallow oval 1½-quart baking dish. Roll pâte brisée out on lightly floured surface to oval slightly larger than baking dish. Cover dish with pastry, pressing against edges to seal. Trim excess pastry and reroll on lightly floured surface. Cut out decorative leaves and arrange over casserole. Bake until top is lightly browned, about 20 minutes.

🍒 Braising and Poaching

Ragout of Lamb à la Grecque

This flavorful dish can be prepared up to 3 days ahead and reheated. It also freezes well. Four cups cooked rice pilaf tossed with 1 cup minced fresh parsley and 2 tablespoons minced fresh mint makes a delightful accompaniment.

6 to 8 servings

1 large eggplant, peeled and cut into 1-inch cubes
Salt

6 to 8 tablespoons olive oil
1 tablespoon butter
3 pounds lean boned lamb shoulder, cubed and patted dry
Salt and freshly ground pepper
All purpose flour
Pinch of sugar

2 cups minced onion
3 garlic cloves, minced
1 28-ounce can Italian plum tomatoes, thoroughly drained and chopped

1 tablespoon tomato paste
1 large sprig fresh oregano (preferably Greek with flowers)
1 bay leaf
1 teaspoon ground cumin
2 cups lamb *or* beef stock

1 tablespoon arrowroot, dissolved in small amount of lamb *or* beef stock
2 tablespoons minced fresh oregano
2 garlic cloves, crushed
½ cup Greek black olives, pitted and halved (optional)
Finely minced fresh parsley (garnish)

Arrange eggplant in single layer on double thickness of paper towels. Sprinkle with salt and let drain 1 hour. Rinse, dry thoroughly and set aside.

Position rack in center of oven and preheat to 350°F. Heat some of oil and butter in heavy 12-inch skillet over medium-high heat. Add lamb in batches *(do not crowd)* and brown on all sides, removing with slotted spoon and adding oil and butter to skillet as necessary. Return all meat to skillet and season with salt and pepper. Sprinkle lightly with flour and sugar and sauté, shaking pan constantly, until lamb is glazed, about 2 to 3 minutes. Transfer to heatproof casserole using slotted spoon.

Add a little more oil and butter to skillet. Add onion and minced garlic and sauté until vegetables are soft and lightly browned, scraping up any browned bits clinging to bottom of skillet, about 2 to 3 minutes. Add tomatoes, tomato paste, oregano sprig, bay leaf and cumin and bring to boil. Pour over lamb. Blend in stock. Cover and braise until lamb is just fork tender, about 1½ hours.

Meanwhile, heat more olive oil in heavy 10-inch skillet over medium-high heat. Add eggplant and sauté until nicely browned on all sides. Transfer to colander or paper towels to drain.

Remove lamb from baking dish using slotted spoon. Strain pan juices through fine sieve. Return to baking dish and place over high direct heat. Whisk in dissolved arrowroot, mixing constantly until sauce heavily coats spoon. Reduce heat and add minced oregano and crushed garlic. Return lamb to casserole. Add eggplant and olives and heat through. Season to taste with salt and pepper. Sprinkle with minced fresh parsley just before serving.

Moroccan Lamb Tajine with Dates

A green salad with black olives, flat bread and a light red wine such as a Beaujolais are all you need to complement this exquisite dish.

6 to 8 servings

1 3-pound lamb shoulder, well trimmed and cut into bite-size pieces
Salt and freshly ground pepper
¼ cup (½ stick) butter
2 medium-size yellow onions, finely chopped
2 cups beef stock
½ teaspoon saffron threads, crushed, *or* ¼ teaspoon ground saffron

1 small cinnamon stick
1 tablespoon honey
1 teaspoon cinnamon
1 cup pitted dates, halved
½ cup toasted whole almonds (toast 10 minutes at 350°F)
2 teaspoons sesame seed

Pat lamb dry. Season with salt and pepper. Melt butter in heavy large skillet or Dutch oven over medium-high heat. Add lamb and onions and sauté until onion is soft and meat is brown. Heat ½ cup beef stock in small saucepan over low heat. Blend in saffron and stir to dissolve. Add saffron mixture to lamb with remaining stock and cinnamon stick and bring to boil. Reduce heat, cover and simmer until lamb is tender, about 1½ hours.

Remove lamb from skillet using slotted spoon; discard cinnamon stick. Stir in honey and cinnamon and simmer 5 more minutes. Return lamb to pan. Add dates and continue simmering until dates are plump, about 5 minutes. Arrange mixture on serving platter. Sprinkle with almonds and sesame seed and serve.

Near Eastern Lamb Filling

Makes 8 sandwiches

3 tablespoons vegetable *or* olive oil
2 large garlic cloves, minced
1 large onion, chopped
2 tablespoons chopped fresh parsley
1½ pounds lean boneless lamb, cut into 1-inch cubes
2 medium tomatoes, peeled, seeded and diced
2 tablespoons fresh lemon juice
1 tablespoon red wine vinegar

1½ teaspoons salt
⅛ teaspoon ground red pepper
⅛ teaspoon ground cumin
Freshly ground pepper
½ cup water *or* stock (optional)
1 cup garbanzo beans (chick-peas), drained and rinsed

Shredded lettuce (garnish)
Sliced tomato (garnish)

Heat oil in medium skillet over medium heat. Add garlic and onion and sauté until translucent. Add parsley and cook until wilted. Add lamb and brown on all sides. Stir in tomatoes, lemon juice, vinegar and seasoning. Cover and simmer until meat is almost tender, about 35 minutes (add water if necessary to keep meat from burning). Stir in beans and continue cooking 10 minutes.

Serve in Syrian bread pockets and garnish with lettuce and tomato.

Parisian Lamb Stew with White Beans

If you prefer a thicker stew, puree some of the beans and reblend into stew.

6 to 8 servings

3 cups dried white pea (navy) beans
4 pounds boneless lamb stew meat, patted dry
Salt and freshly ground pepper
¼ cup olive oil
2 onions, chopped
4 garlic cloves, minced
2 tablespoons all purpose flour
4 cups chicken *or* beef stock
1 bouquet garni (bay leaf, parsley, celery leaves, ½ teaspoon dried thyme and 1 strip lemon peel, tied together in a cheesecloth bag)

2 tomatoes, peeled, seeded and chopped
1 tablespoon soy sauce
Juice of 1 lemon
1 teaspoon dried rosemary *or* thyme
2 parsley sprigs
¼ cup minced fresh parsley

Place beans in large pot and cover with salted water. Bring to boil over high heat. Cook 2 minutes. Remove from heat, cover and let stand 1 hour. Drain well. Cover beans with fresh water. Cover and simmer until tender, at least 1 hour. Drain beans thoroughly.

Season lamb with salt and pepper. Heat oil in large Dutch oven or heavy large saucepan over medium-high heat. Add lamb in batches and brown on all sides. Remove lamb from saucepan using slotted spoon. Reduce heat to low, add onions and garlic to same saucepan and cook 2 minutes. Add flour and cook until well browned, stirring constantly. Blend in stock, bouquet garni, tomatoes, soy sauce, lemon juice, rosemary and parsley sprigs. Return lamb to saucepan. Add beans and bring to boil. Reduce heat, cover and simmer until meat is tender, about 1½ to 2 hours. Skim fat from sauce. Discard bouquet garni. Season to taste with salt and pepper. Sprinkle with minced fresh parsley and serve.

Braised Lamb with Garlic and Herbs

Serve this dish with rice or orzo.

6 servings

¼ cup olive oil
3 to 4 pounds boneless lamb shoulder, cut into 1½-inch cubes
Salt and freshly ground pepper
14 medium garlic cloves, unpeeled
3 medium shallots, finely chopped
4 medium fennel bulbs, tough outer layer discarded, strings peeled off, cored and coarsely chopped
1 cup dry vermouth *or* dry white wine

1 cup beef stock
2 tablespoons fresh lemon juice
6 juniper berries, crushed, *or* 2 tablespoons gin
½ teaspoon dried thyme

1 tablespoon minced fresh parsley *or* fresh mint sprig
1 lemon, thinly sliced (garnish)

Heat oil in Dutch oven over medium-high heat. Pat lamb dry. Add to pan in batches *(do not crowd)* and brown on all sides. Remove lamb and season lightly with salt and pepper. Reduce heat to medium. Add garlic, shallots and half of fennel to pan and stir frequently until just beginning to soften, about 5 minutes. Pour in vermouth and stock. Increase heat to high and stir, scraping up any browned bits. Return lamb to Dutch oven with lemon juice, juniper berries and thyme and bring to boil. Reduce heat, cover and simmer gently until lamb is tender, about 1 to 1½ hours, adding remaining fennel 15 minutes before end of cooking time. Skim fat from surface.

Remove lamb and fennel from pan with slotted spoon. Remove garlic cloves and place in strainer. Press with back of spoon, returning pulp to pan. Bring liquid to boil. Cook until reduced to saucelike consistency. Adjust seasoning. Return lamb and fennel to pan and heat through. Turn into serving dish. Garnish with parsley and lemon slices and serve.

Curried Lamb

6 servings

⅓ cup dried onion
¼ cup warm water
3 tablespoons vegetable oil
2 tablespoons ground coriander
1½ teaspoons ground cumin
1 teaspoon ground cardamom
1 teaspoon ground ginger
1 teaspoon turmeric
½ teaspoon garlic powder
¼ teaspoon freshly ground pepper

⅛ teaspoon ground red pepper
2 pounds boneless leg of lamb *or* lamb stew meat, cut into 1-inch cubes and patted dry
2 cups water *or* lamb *or* beef stock
Salt
¼ cup plain yogurt
1 teaspoon fresh lemon juice
Freshly cooked rice

Soak onion in water until soft, about 5 minutes. Heat oil in large skillet over medium-high heat. Add onion and sauté until golden, about 4 minutes. Reduce heat to low, add spices and stir 1 minute. Add lamb to skillet. Increase heat to medium high and cook, stirring frequently, until meat is evenly browned, 10 to 15 minutes. Add water and salt. Reduce heat to medium, cover and cook until meat is tender, about 20 minutes. Simmer uncovered until sauce thickens, about 20 minutes. Stir in yogurt and lemon juice. Serve immediately over cooked rice.

Deviled Breast of Lamb

2 servings

1 breast of lamb (about 2 pounds)
½ onion, peeled and stuck with 1 whole clove
1 celery stalk, cut into pieces
1 small carrot, cut into pieces
1 garlic clove
1 fresh parsley sprig
½ bay leaf

1 egg, beaten
1 teaspoon Dijon mustard
¼ teaspoon dry mustard
Dash of hot pepper sauce
Pinch of dried oregano
1 cup (about) fine dry breadcrumbs
2 tablespoons (¼ stick) butter
2 tablespoons vegetable oil

Combine lamb, onion, celery, carrot, garlic, parsley and bay leaf in large saucepan or Dutch oven. Add enough salted water to cover. Place over high heat and bring to boil. Let boil 5 minutes. Skim foam from surface. Reduce heat to medium low, cover and simmer until meat is tender, about 1¼ hours. Remove meat (reserve stock for another use) and let stand until cool enough to handle, about 30 minutes. Discard all fat and bone. Transfer meat to plate, cover with another plate and top with weight. Let cool completely. *(Can be prepared ahead to this point, wrapped and frozen. Thaw before proceeding.)*

Cut lamb into bite-size pieces. Combine beaten egg, mustards, hot pepper sauce and oregano in small bowl. Dip meat into egg mixture, then coat lightly with breadcrumbs. Melt butter with oil in large skillet over medium-high heat. Add lamb (in batches if necessary; *do not crowd*) and sauté until crisp and browned on all sides, about 10 minutes. Serve immediately.

Lamb Shanks Provençal

4 servings

4 lamb shanks (about ¾ pound each)
4 medium garlic cloves, slivered
⅓ cup olive oil
2 medium onions, chopped
4 carrots
2 celery stalks, including leaves
2 cups canned Italian plum tomatoes, drained

1 cup dry red wine
1 cup beef stock
1 lemon, halved and seeded
  Bouquet garni (bay leaf, parsley sprig and rosemary sprig, tied together in a cheesecloth bag)

1 teaspoon salt
  Freshly ground pepper

Trim excess fat from lamb shanks and discard. Make small slits in shanks and insert 1 garlic clove in each shank. Heat oil in large skillet over medium-low heat. Add onions. Cover and cook until translucent, stirring occasionally, about 10 minutes. Remove onions with slotted spoon and set aside. Increase heat to high. Add shanks to skillet and brown evenly on all sides, about 10 minutes. Return onions to skillet. Add remaining ingredients except salt and pepper and bring to boil. Reduce heat to low, cover and simmer until shanks are fork tender, about 1 to 1½ hours. Transfer shanks to heated ovenproof serving platter and keep warm while preparing sauce.

Preheat oven to 425°F. Place same skillet over high heat and boil until sauce is slightly thickened and reduced to 3 cups. Discard lemon halves and bouquet garni. Transfer sauce to processor or blender and puree. Season to taste with salt and pepper. Ladle some of sauce over shanks. Transfer remaining sauce to sauceboat and keep warm. Bake lamb shanks until glaze forms, about 15 to 20 minutes. Serve immediately, serving remaining sauce separately.

4 🍐 Pork

No meat appears on our tables in so many guises as pork. Chops, ribs, steaks, scallops, medallions, loins, fillets and roasts; minced and cooked in loaves or patties, or stuffed into sausage casings; offered up as home-style hocks or as gala hams (and don't forget the bacon): Pork cuts and products are so numerous, so varied—so *bountiful*—that it is impossible to dispute the words of the Roman poet Juvenal, who called the pig "the animal born for feasting."

The feast of pork recipes that follows shows off the meat in all its varied forms. Not surprisingly, many of the recipes include fruits or lively spices, which complement pork's robust, slightly sweet flavor. Among recipes for tender cuts best suited to the fast-cooking heat of the grill or frying pan, you will find Grilled Tenderloin (page 88) partnered by a puree of apples and sweet potatoes, and Skewered Barbecue Pork with spicy peanut sauce (page 88). From the oven comes Irish Loin of Pork with Lemon and Herbs (page 91), Roasted Spareribs with Hoisin-Honey Glaze (page 92) and Marinated Pork with Apricots and Pistachio Nuts (page 94). And pork braises and stews here include Provençal Pork in Fennel Cups with anchovies, olives and capers (page 105) and sugar-glazed Chinese Red-cooked Pork Hock (page 109).

Homemade pork sausages are represented here in a delightful range of international recipes, each gaining special flair from the distinctive ingredients and seasonings of its cuisine. English-style Cumberland Sausage (page 90) has the savor of allspice and sage. French Champagne Sausage (page 111), flavored with Champagne, walnuts, and aromatic herbs is enlivened with rich Sauce Piquante. And there is a fresh Italian sausage here—one subtley seasoned with fennel seed, chilies, marjoram, and just a touch of garlic (page 112).

When you shop for pork, choose meat that is firm to the touch and moist, with bright white fat. Pork loin should be pale pink, the shoulder and leg cuts slightly deeper in color.

❧ Grilling and Broiling

Grilled Tenderloin of Pork

6 servings

Pork can also be broiled. Tie two ⅛-inch-thick slices of pancetta (Italian dry-cured unsmoked bacon) lengthwise onto tenderloins and marinate according to recipe instructions. Cook pork in preheated broiler 6 inches from heat source about 15 to 20 minutes, turning frequently.

6 servings

½ cup olive oil
1 garlic clove

3 sprigs fresh rosemary

2 1-pound pork tenderloins

Apple and Sweet Potato Puree (see following recipe)

Combine olive oil and garlic in jar. Cover and let stand overnight.

Pour olive oil into baking dish. Add rosemary. Place pork in dish and turn to coat all sides. Set pork aside at room temperature to marinate for 1½ hours, turning occasionally.

Prepare indoor grill. Transfer pork to grill and cook, basting occasionally with remaining marinade, about 12 to 15 minutes, turning frequently. Slice into medallions. Spoon puree onto plates. Top with pork and serve.

Apple and Sweet Potato Puree

1 pound sweet potatoes (about 2 medium)

8 tablespoons (1 stick) butter
1½ pounds Pippin or Granny Smith apples, peeled, cored and sliced

1 tablespoon fresh lemon juice
1½ teaspoons salt
2 to 3 pieces preserved ginger
½ teaspoon cinnamon

Preheat oven to 375°F. Bake potatoes until tender, about 50 minutes. Discard skin; reserve pulp.

Melt 1 tablespoon butter in large skillet over medium heat. Add apples, cover and cook until soft and mushy, about 12 minutes, stirring occasionally. Transfer apples to processor. Add sweet potatoes, lemon juice, salt, ginger, cinnamon and remaining 7 tablespoons butter and mix in processor using on/off turns, until smooth. Serve hot.

Skewered Barbecued Pork (Saté Babi)

Makes about 18 skewers

1 small onion, chopped
1 piece fresh ginger (about 1 inch long), peeled and minced
1 garlic clove, minced
½ cup Indonesian Soy Sauce (see following recipes) *or* commercial kecap manis

2 tablespoons fresh lime juice
1 pound lean, boneless pork, cut into ½-inch cubes

Peanut Sauce (kacang saus) (see following recipes)

Combine onion, ginger, garlic, soy sauce and lime juice in bowl. Add pork and mix well. Cover and marinate 2 hours, tossing occasionally with fork.

Prepare charcoal (or use broiler). Remove pork from marinade and thread on wooden or bamboo skewers (5 or 6 cubes to each 6- to 8-inch skewer). Grill or broil slowly, turning frequently and basting with marinade, until done, about 8 to 10 minutes. Serve with Peanut Sauce for dipping.

Stuffed Pork Chops from Bern

Clockwise from top right:
White Bean One-pot, Prince's Pot, Butcher's
One-pot with Sauerkraut

Victor Scocozza

*Pork Steaks with Cardamom
and Fresh Grapes*

Victor Scocozza

*Roasted Spareribs with
Hoisin-Honey Glaze*

Ragout of Pork
with Rosemary

Indonesian Soy Sauce (Kecap Manis)

A common ingredient in Balinese and Indonesian cuisine. Both commercial and homemade versions will keep 2 to 3 months tightly covered in the refrigerator.

Makes about 3 cups

1 cup firmly packed dark brown sugar
1 cup water
1 cup soy sauce
7 tablespoons dark molasses
1 teaspoon grated fresh ginger
½ teaspoon ground coriander
½ teaspoon freshly ground pepper

Combine sugar and water in 2-quart saucepan. Bring to simmer over medium heat, stirring just until sugar dissolves. Increase heat to high and continue cooking until syrup reaches 200°F on candy thermometer, about 5 minutes. Reduce heat to low, stir in remaining ingredients and simmer 3 minutes.

Peanut Sauce (Kacang Saus)

This sauce, or variations of it, shows up in many Indonesian dishes, such as the pork and lamb satés and Gado-Gado. It is important to use Spanish peanuts, which are the type grown in Bali.

Makes about 2 cups

1½ cups salted Spanish peanuts with skins (not dry roasted) *or* peanut butter

1 tablespoon peanut oil
¼ cup chopped onion
4 garlic cloves, minced
1½ cups canned coconut cream
1½ to 2 teaspoons crushed chili paste (sambal oelek), dried red pepper flakes *or* chili powder

1 teaspoon ground ginger
¼ teaspoon ground cumin
3 tablespoons fresh lemon juice
4 to 5 tablespoons Indonesian Soy Sauce or commercial kecap manis (see preceding recipe)

Place peanuts in processor or blender and mix to paste or butter, stopping to scrape down sides as necessary.

Heat oil in small saucepan. Add onion and garlic and sauté about 1 minute. Stirring constantly, add coconut cream, chili paste, ginger, cumin, lemon juice and soy sauce and bring to boil. Whisk in peanut butter and cook, stirring constantly, until sauce is thickened, about 3 to 5 minutes.

Barbecued Bones

After removing bones from pork roasts or chops, store in freezer to barbecue later for family nibbling.

4 servings

¼ cup apricot jam
¼ cup Dijon mustard
¼ cup wine vinegar *or* cider vinegar
1 large garlic clove, minced
Pinch of ground red pepper
4 pounds (about) meaty pork bones, spareribs or back ribs

Prepare barbecue with medium-low coals. Mix jam, mustard, vinegar, garlic and ground red pepper in small bowl. Set aside. Grill bones 45 minutes, turning occasionally. Brush with glaze. Continue cooking until bones are crisp and brown, brushing with glaze every 10 minutes and turning occasionally, about 35 minutes. (Bones can also be broiled. Arrange on rack in broiler pan. Broil 6 inches from heat source, brushing with apricot-mustard glaze.) Serve hot or warm.

🍎 Sautéing and Deep-frying

Cumberland Sausage

This mixture can also be used to fill pork sausage casings.

Makes 12 patties

1 pound pork shoulder
½ pound veal stew meat
⅔ cup cracker meal
1 egg
1½ teaspoons milk
½ teaspoon salt
¼ teaspoon allspice
¼ teaspoon ground sage

¼ teaspoon onion powder
¼ teaspoon freshly ground white pepper
¼ cup chopped fresh parsley

2 tablespoons (¼ stick) butter
2 tablespoons vegetable oil

Grind pork and veal together twice, using fine blade of meat grinder. Combine cracker meal, egg, milk, salt, allspice, sage, onion powder and pepper in large bowl and mix well. Add ground meat and parsley and blend thoroughly. Divide mixture evenly into 12 patties.

Melt butter with oil in large skillet over medium-high heat. Add patties (in batches if necessary; *do not crowd*) and fry until golden brown, turning once, about 2 to 3 minutes per side. Drain on paper towels. Serve immediately.

German-style Schnitzel

6 servings

6 boneless pork loin cutlets (about 2 pounds total), trimmed

½ cup all purpose flour
2 teaspoons seasoned salt
½ teaspoon freshly ground pepper
2 eggs
¼ cup milk
1½ cups fresh breadcrumbs
2 teaspoons paprika
6 tablespoons vegetable shortening

2 tablespoons all purpose flour
½ teaspoon dried dillweed
1½ cups chicken stock
1 cup sour cream, room temperature

Place cutlets between 2 sheets of waxed paper and flatten to ¼- to ½-inch thickness. Cut small slits around edges of pork to prevent curling. Set aside.

Combine ½ cup flour and salt and pepper in shallow bowl or on sheet of waxed paper. Beat eggs with milk in another shallow bowl. Mix crumbs and paprika in small bowl or on another sheet of waxed paper.

Melt 3 tablespoons shortening in large skillet over medium heat. Dip cutlets in flour, then into egg mixture. Coat with crumbs, covering completely. Add 3 cutlets to skillet and sauté on both sides until coating is golden brown and meat is no longer pink, about 3 to 5 minutes per side. Transfer to platter and keep warm. Repeat with remaining shortening and cutlets.

Combine remaining flour with dillweed. Add to skillet, scraping up any browned bits clinging to bottom of pan. Add stock, stirring constantly until well blended. Stir in sour cream and cook until heated through. Spoon over cutlets or serve separately.

Five-Spice Meat

*2 main-course servings
or 4 servings as part of
multicourse Chinese meal*

1 pound pork tenderloin, cut into
  1-inch cubes
2 tablespoons water
1½ tablespoons dark soy sauce
1½ tablespoons light soy sauce
1 teaspoon five-spice powder
½ teaspoon cornstarch
¼ teaspoon freshly ground white
  pepper

⅛ teaspoon Chinese cooking wine
  or dry white wine

2 cups stemmed spinach leaves
10 tomato slices

1 egg, beaten to blend
3 tablespoons cornstarch
  Vegetable oil (for deep frying)

Slightly flatten pork cubes with side of cleaver. Mix with water, soy sauces, five-spice powder, ½ teaspoon cornstarch, pepper and wine and marinate 1 hour at room temperature or 3 hours in refrigerator, stirring occasionally.

Cover serving platter with spinach. Arrange tomato around edge.

Vigorously mix egg and 3 tablespoons cornstarch into meat mixture for 1 minute. Heat oil in wok or heavy large skillet over high heat to 350°F. Reduce heat to medium high. Add pork and deep fry until golden brown, 10 to 15 minutes, turning occasionally. Drain on paper towels. Mound pork in center of platter. Serve immediately.

🍎 *Roasting and Baking*

Irish Loin of Pork with Lemon and Herbs

6 to 8 servings

1 5- to 6-pound boneless pork loin
½ cup chopped fresh parsley
¼ cup minced onion
¼ cup finely grated lemon peel
1 tablespoon chopped fresh basil
3 medium garlic cloves, crushed

½ cup plus 3 tablespoons olive oil

¾ cup dry Sherry
  Fresh parsley (garnish)
  Lemon slices (garnish)

Pat pork dry. Score well with sharp knife. Combine parsley, onion, peel, basil and garlic in small bowl. Whisk in ½ cup oil. Rub into pork. Wrap in foil and refrigerate overnight.

Let pork stand at room temperature 1 hour before roasting. Preheat oven to 350°F. Brush pork with remaining 3 tablespoons olive oil. Set on rack in shallow pan. Roast until meat thermometer inserted in thickest part of meat registers 170°F, about 2½ hours. Set meat aside. Degrease pan juices. Blend Sherry into pan juices. Cook over low heat 2 minutes. Pour into sauceboat. Transfer pork to platter. Garnish with fresh parsley and lemon slices. Serve sauce separately.

Indonesian Spareribs (Babi Asam)

Have your butcher saw the whole rib rack into 3 pieces. Served hot from the oven or at room temperature, these spicy ribs are great with cocktails or as part of an oriental menu.

6 appetizer servings

12 ounces dried tamarind pulp* with seeds
2 cups water, at boiling point
6 small dried chilies, stemmed and seeded
¾ cup unsweetened coconut
¾ cup water
3 tablespoons sugar

3 tablespoons soy sauce
3 tablespoons fresh lime juice
6 large garlic cloves, crushed
¾ teaspoon ground coriander
2½ to 3 pounds pork spareribs, sawed crosswise into 3 strips and trimmed

Salt

Combine tamarind and 2 cups boiling water in small bowl, breaking up pulp with fork. Soak 1 hour.

Grind chilies in processor or blender. Add remaining ingredients except spareribs, salt and tamarind mixture. Pour tamarind through fine strainer into processor or blender, pressing through as much pulp as possible. Blend mixture 1 minute. Arrange spareribs in shallow glass dish. Pour marinade over, turning ribs to coat evenly. Refrigerate 6 to 8 hours, turning ribs occasionally.

Preheat oven to 325°F. Pat ribs dry (reserve marinade). Sprinkle ribs lightly with salt. Arrange on rack set over large shallow roasting pan containing 1 cup water. Roast 30 minutes. Turn ribs and brush with marinade. Continue cooking, brushing frequently with marinade and turning, until evenly browned, about 1 hour. (Ribs can also be barbecued over medium-hot coals.) Cut ribs apart and serve them hot.

*Available at Indian and oriental markets and specialty food stores.

Roasted Spareribs with Hoisin-Honey Glaze

Serve with a good Mexican beer.

6 to 8 servings

1 12-ounce bottle beer
¾ cup hoisin sauce*
¾ cup honey
¾ cup soy sauce
¾ cup minced green onion

3 tablespoons minced fresh ginger *or* 1 tablespoon ground

9 pounds lean pork spareribs

Combine all ingredients except ribs in medium saucepan over low heat and cook 5 minutes to blend flavors. *(Glaze can be prepared ahead to this point, cooled, covered and refrigerated. Reheat before proceeding with recipe.)*

About 2 hours before serving time, position racks in upper and lower thirds of oven and preheat to 350°F. Brush ribs with glaze. Set in 2 large roasting pans and arrange on racks. Roast until well browned, about 1½ to 1¾ hours, turning ribs every 30 minutes and basting with glaze. Transfer to work surface and cut between ribs. Arrange on heated platter and serve immediately.

*Available in oriental markets.

Crown Roast of Pork with Breaded Cauliflower, Grilled Tomatoes and Sauce Morilles

8 to 10 servings

1 6- to 8-pound pork loin, frenched
  and formed into crown
6 strips fresh side pork *or* pork
  back fat

¼ cup (½ stick) butter
1 cup fine dry breadcrumbs
  Salt and freshly ground pepper

1 medium cauliflower
1 medium cauliflower, broken into
  florets

5 ripe tomatoes, cored and halved
  horizontally
2½ teaspoons butter
1 sprig fresh rosemary, oregano *or*
  parsley, chopped
  Salt and freshly ground pepper

Sauce Morilles
¼ cup (½ stick) butter
12 to 15 dried morels, soaked in
  cold water until soft, rinsed
  thoroughly, drained and finely
  chopped
2 cups brown stock
2 tablespoons cornstarch
2 tablespoons Cognac

  Watercress (garnish)

Preheat oven to 325°F. Cover tips of pork bones with pieces of aluminum foil to prevent burning. Wrap pork strips around meat to retain moistness. Transfer pork to roasting pan and cook 35 minutes per pound.

Meanwhile, melt ¼ cup butter in small skillet over medium heat. Stir in breadcrumbs and cook 3 to 4 minutes. Season with salt and pepper to taste.

About 15 minutes before roast is ready, add whole cauliflower to large saucepan half filled with boiling salted water. Let cook 5 minutes. Add cauliflower florets and continue cooking until crisp-tender, about 9 to 10 minutes. Drain well. Transfer roast to serving platter. Place whole cauliflower in center of roast and florets around base. Pat breadcrumbs over top of whole cauliflower. Freeze juices in roasting pan or other shallow container for 10 minutes; discard fat.

Increase oven temperature to 400°F. Arrange tomato halves in shallow baking dish. Dot each with ¼ teaspoon butter and sprinkle with rosemary. Season with salt and pepper. Bake until tomatoes are soft but still hold their shape, about 12 minutes. Arrange tomatoes on platter between cauliflower florets. Turn off oven. When temperature is reduced, return roast to oven to keep warm.

For sauce morilles: Melt ¼ cup butter in medium saucepan over medium-high heat. Add morels and sauté about 2 to 3 minutes. Set aside. Add brown stock and cornstarch to reserved pan juices. Place over medium-high heat and cook, scraping up any browned bits. Reduce heat and let simmer until thickened. Stir in Cognac and morels and heat through. Transfer to heated sauceboat.

Arrange watercress between tomatoes and cauliflower florets. Serve roast immediately with warm sauce.

Marinated Pork with Apricots and Pistachios

This festive pork dish is excellent party fare. Serve with a tart saffron rice salad, braised carrots and green beans, roasted potatoes and a dry white wine or imported dry cider.

For a large party, use a 14- to 16-pound uncured boned ham (16 to 24 servings). Double the marinade and increase the stuffing by ¼. Roast 1 hour at 400°F. Reduce oven temperature to 350°F and continue roasting until meat thermometer inserted in thickest part of ham registers 155°F, about 3 hours.

6 to 8 servings

Marinade
- 2 cups dry white wine
- 2 cups apple cider*
- ½ cup apple cider vinegar
- ½ cup Calvados *or* applejack
- 5 whole cloves
- 4 garlic cloves, crushed
- 3 cardamom pods, crushed
- 2 cinnamon sticks, broken
- 1 onion, sliced
- 1 tablespoon whole black peppercorns, crushed
- 1 tablespoon whole allspice, crushed
- 1½ teaspoons ground ginger
- 1 4- to 5-pound pork sirloin roast, boned and left unrolled *or* ½ whole fresh (uncured) ham, boned and left unrolled

- ¼ cup (½ stick) unsalted butter
- 9 green onions, minced
- 3 large garlic cloves, minced
- 1 medium onion, minced
- 9 ounces dried apricots, chopped
- ¾ cup shelled pistachios
- ¾ cup minced fresh parsley
- 6 tablespoons pine nuts, toasted (toast 10 minutes at 350°F)
- 1½ tablespoons finely grated lemon peel
- 1 tablespoon (scant) cider vinegar
  Salt and freshly ground pepper

Lemon leaves *or* other greens (garnish)

For marinade: Combine first 12 ingredients in large bowl. Add meat, turning to coat. Cover and refrigerate 1 to 2 days, turning meat every 12 hours.

Melt ¼ cup butter in heavy large skillet over medium-high heat. Add green onions, garlic and onion and sauté 3 minutes. Remove from heat and stir in apricots, pistachios, parsley, pine nuts, lemon peel, cider vinegar and salt and pepper, blending well. Cover and refrigerate. *(Can be prepared up to 2 days ahead.)*

Preheat oven to 400°F. Remove meat from marinade and pat dry with paper towels; strain and reserve marinade. Set meat on work surface, fat side down, and flatten slightly. Spread apricot mixture evenly over meat, leaving ½- to 1-inch border all around. Roll up lengthwise and tie at 2-inch intervals with heavy string. (If using ham with skin intact, score in diamond pattern before tying.) Set meat skin side down in large deep roasting pan. Pour about 3 cups strained marinade into pan and roast 1 hour. Reduce oven temperature to 350°F and continue roasting, basting frequently with remaining marinade, until meat thermometer inserted in thickest part of meat registers 155°F, about 1¼ hours. Transfer to heated serving platter and keep warm. (Cooked ham can be kept warm in low oven for about 1 hour. Tent lightly with foil.) Degrease pan juices. Transfer to saucepan and boil over high heat until thickened and reduced. Surround meat with lemon leaves and carve at table. Serve sauce separately.

*English, French or Canadian hard cider can be substituted for wine and cider.

Gaelic Stuffed Pork Tenderloin

2 to 3 servings

1 1-pound pork tenderloin

2 tablespoons (¼ stick) butter
½ cup chopped onion
1 cup fresh breadcrumbs
¼ cup minced fresh parsley

¼ teaspoon dried sage
¼ teaspoon dried rosemary
   Salt and freshly ground pepper
1 egg, beaten
1 slice bacon, cut in half

Split tenderloin lengthwise partially through to butterfly. Open and pound flat between 2 sheets of waxed paper.

Preheat oven to 350°F. Melt butter in small skillet over medium heat. Add onion and sauté until tender. Stir in breadcrumbs and continue cooking until slightly crisp. Add parsley, sage, rosemary and salt and pepper. Cool. Add enough egg to moisten. Spread stuffing on half of meat, leaving ¼-inch border on all sides. Fold to close. Place bacon over top and tie with string. Transfer to baking pan and roast until meat registers 170°F, about 1 to 1½ hours.

Chinese Barbecued Spareribs

Serve hot or chilled.

4 servings

4 pounds pork spareribs, cracked at
   2- to 3-inch lengths and separated
2 medium-size yellow onions, sliced
¼ cup plus 1 tablespoon soy sauce
¼ cup plus 1 tablespoon water

3 tablespoons hoisin sauce*
2 tablespoons light honey
1 teaspoon five-spice powder
⅛ teaspoon ground ginger

Arrange ribs in shallow roasting pan. Combine remaining ingredients in medium bowl and mix well. Pour over ribs, turning to coat completely. Let ribs marinate in refrigerator at least 8 hours or overnight.

Preheat oven to 325°F. Bake ribs in sauce, turning 3 or 4 times, for 1½ hours. (Sauce remaining in roasting pan after cooking can be reduced over high heat and used to glaze ribs.)

*Available in oriental markets.

Baked Smoked Pork and Vegetables with Chive Sauce

Accompany this robust platter with crusty loaves of bread and a dry Riesling or dark German beer.

4 to 5 servings

1 2- to 2¼-pound boneless smoked pork butt roll *or* 1¾- to 2-pound slab of Canadian bacon, cut into 7 or 8 slices
¼ cup (½ stick) butter
10 to 12 small brussels sprouts, trimmed (½ pound)
3 medium leeks (white part only), cut into 1¼-inch rounds
3 medium carrots, coarsely sliced
1 1-pound rutabaga, peeled and cut into ½-inch cubes
Salt and freshly ground pepper

1½ to 1¾ pounds cabbage, cut into 4 to 6 wedges
¼ cup (½ stick) butter, melted

Chive Sauce
¼ cup (½ stick) butter
¼ cup snipped fresh chives
2 tablespoons all purpose flour
1 teaspoon tomato paste
2 cups half and half
½ teaspoon salt
2 egg yolks, room temperature

Preheat oven to 375°F. Brown pork in 12-inch skillet over medium heat, about 5 minutes on each side. Transfer slices to 9 × 13-inch baking dish. Add ¼ cup butter to skillet and let melt. Add brussels sprouts, leeks, carrots and rutabaga and toss gently until coated with butter. Cook 3 minutes, stirring constantly. Spoon vegetables and juices over pork. Sprinkle with salt and pepper to taste. Cover and bake 20 minutes.

Arrange cabbage wedges over vegetables and brush with half of melted butter. Re-cover, reduce oven to 350°F and bake 25 minutes. Brush cabbage with remaining melted butter. Re-cover and continue baking until vegetables are tender when pierced with fork, about 35 minutes.

For chive sauce: Melt ¼ cup butter in heavy small saucepan over medium-high heat. Stir in chives and bring to boil. Let boil 30 seconds. Reduce heat to medium, add flour and stir 3 minutes. Blend in tomato paste. Gradually add half and half and salt. Increase heat and stir until mixture thickens and simmers. Reduce heat to medium and simmer 2 minutes, stirring constantly. Beat yolks to blend in small bowl. Beat ⅔ cup chive mixture into yolks several drops at a time. Gradually add yolk mixture back into saucepan, blending well. Reduce heat to medium and cook 1 minute, stirring constantly; *do not boil*. Season with salt if desired. Serve immediately as an accompaniment to pork and vegetables.

Pork Baby Back Ribs

6 servings

6 to 7½ pounds pork baby back ribs

Sauce
1 29-ounce can tomato sauce
2 cups white vinegar
10 ounces canned pineapple chunks, quartered
½ cup firmly packed brown sugar
½ cup sugar

¼ cup teriyaki sauce
2 tablespoons soy sauce
2 tablespoons honey
2 tablespoons Worcestershire sauce
1 teaspoon dried onion
1 teaspoon garlic salt
½ teaspoon chili powder
2 tablespoons cornstarch
2 tablespoons water

Preheat oven to 400°F. Arrange ribs in single layer in shallow pans. Cover with foil and bake until tender, about 1 hour.

For sauce: Combine remaining ingredients except cornstarch and water in large saucepan and bring to boil over medium-high heat. Reduce heat and simmer

30 minutes. Mix cornstarch with water in small bowl to form a smooth paste. Stir into sauce. Continue cooking 5 minutes longer.

Remove ribs from pans. Pour off all fat. Reduce oven temperature to 350°F. Return ribs to pans, meaty side down. Brush generously with sauce and bake, basting frequently, 15 minutes. Turn ribs over and continue baking and basting until ribs are browned and crispy, about 30 minutes.

French-Canadian Meat Pie (Tourtière)

Serve this hearty Canadian favorite for a 1-dish winter dinner.

6 to 8 servings

Cheddar Crust
1½ cups all purpose flour
⅓ cup grated aged cheddar cheese
½ teaspoon salt
¼ cup (½ stick) unsalted butter, well chilled and cut into pieces
¼ cup lard *or* vegetable shortening
¼ cup ice water, or more

Filling
3 tablespoons vegetable oil
2 medium onions, minced
2 medium garlic cloves, minced
1½ pounds lean ground pork
2 medium tomatoes, peeled, seeded and finely chopped
¼ cup water
½ teaspoon cinnamon
½ teaspoon dried savory
¼ teaspoon celery seed
⅛ teaspoon ground cloves
½ cup fresh breadcrumbs
Salt and freshly ground pepper

1 tablespoon Dijon mustard
1 egg beaten with 2 tablespoons whipping cream (glaze)

For cheddar crust: Combine flour, cheese and salt in large bowl. Cut in butter and lard until mixture resembles coarse meal. Blend in ¼ cup ice water just until dough holds together, adding more water if necessary. Divide dough in half. Shape into balls. Wrap in plastic. Chill while preparing filling.

For filling: Heat oil in heavy large skillet over medium-low heat. Add onions and garlic. Cover and cook until translucent, about 10 minutes, stirring occasionally. Add pork and cook until no longer pink, mashing frequently with fork. Mix in tomatoes, water, cinnamon, savory, celery seed and cloves. Reduce heat to medium low and simmer until most of liquid is absorbed, about 30 minutes. Stir in breadcrumbs and salt and pepper; cool.

Roll 1 portion of dough out on lightly floured surface into ⅛-inch-thick round. Gather dough up on rolling pin and unroll into 10-inch deep-dish metal pie pan. Brush bottom with mustard. Spoon filling into crust. Roll remaining dough out on lightly floured surface into ⅛-inch-thick round. Drape pastry over dish, crimping edges to seal and trimming excess. Reroll dough scraps and cut out leaf shapes. Cut 8 vents in decorative flower-petal pattern in top crust to allow steam to escape. Brush pastry with glaze. Arrange pastry leaves atop crust and brush with glaze. *(Can be prepared 1 day ahead. Cover and refrigerate.)*

Preheat oven to 425°F. Bake pie 10 minutes. Reduce oven temperature to 350°F and continue baking until golden brown, about 35 minutes. (If top browns too quickly, drape loosely with aluminum foil.) Serve hot, warm or at room temperature.

Mediterranean Ham-Potato Torte

Serve this at your first spring picnic—it's great hot or cold. A salad with fresh fruit for dessert would complete the menu nicely. Accompany with a dry rosé from Côtes de Provence.

8 to 10 servings

Pastry
- 1 pound boiling potatoes, peeled and quartered
- 1 cup all purpose flour
- ½ cup plus 2 tablespoons (1¼ sticks) unsalted butter, cut into ½-inch pieces and slightly softened
- 1 teaspoon coarse salt

Filling
- 2 tablespoons olive oil
- 1 cup chopped onion
- 1½ teaspoons minced garlic
- 3 cups peeled, seeded and chopped fresh tomatoes (preferably Italian plum tomatoes)
- ½ cup dry white wine
- 1 cup diced cooked ham
- ¾ cup shredded Gruyère cheese
- 1 6-ounce jar marinated artichoke hearts, drained, patted dry and halved
- 2 eggs
- 1 egg yolk
- 2½ tablespoons chopped fresh basil
- 1 teaspoon coarse salt
- ¼ teaspoon freshly ground pepper

For pastry: Bring large amount of water to rapid boil. Add potatoes and cook until very tender, about 20 minutes. Drain well. While still hot, transfer potatoes to food mill set over large bowl and puree in batches; *do not use processor.* Reserve ½ cup potato puree for filling. Let remaining puree cool.

Add flour, butter and salt to cooled potato puree. Using pastry blender, cut mixture into pieces as small as possible; *do not use processor.* Continue cutting until mixture forms ball. Turn dough out onto generously floured surface. Knead twice. Pat or lightly roll dough into 12-inch circle, turning dough in flour occasionally to prevent sticking. Carefully transfer dough to 9-inch springform pan. Gently pat dough into bottom and 1¾ inches up sides. Cover surface of pastry shell with plastic wrap and refrigerate shell until ready to add filling.

For filling: Heat oil in heavy large skillet over high heat. Add onion and garlic and cook until onion is softened, 3 to 5 minutes, stirring frequently. Blend in tomatoes and wine. Reduce heat and simmer gently until all liquid has evaporated, about 45 minutes, stirring occasionally. Let sauce cool.

Preheat oven to 375°F. Mix ham, ½ cup Gruyère, artichokes, eggs, yolk, basil, salt, pepper and reserved potato puree in medium bowl. Blend mixture into tomato sauce. Pour filling into pastry shell. Sprinkle remaining ¼ cup Gruyère over top. Set tart on baking sheet. Bake until filling is set and crust is golden brown, about 55 minutes. Serve warm or at room temperature.

Cabbage and Ham Tart

8 to 10 servings

Pastry
1½ cups all purpose flour
 1 teaspoon coarse salt
 ½ cup (1 stick) unsalted butter,
     well chilled and cut into ½-inch
     pieces
 2 tablespoons vegetable shortening,
     well chilled and cut into ½-inch
     pieces
 1 egg
 3 to 4 tablespoons cold water

Filling
 3 cups coarsely chopped cabbage

 2 tablespoons (¼ stick) unsalted
     butter

 1 cup whipping cream
 1 cup sliced cooked ham, cut into
     ¼ × ¼ × 1-inch strips
 2 eggs
 ⅓ cup chopped walnuts
 ¼ cup chopped fresh parsley
 2 teaspoons grated lemon peel
 ¾ teaspoon coarse salt
 ¼ teaspoon freshly ground pepper

 1 egg yolk blended with 1 teaspoon
     water

 1 cup chopped onion
 1 tablespoon all purpose flour
 2 tablespoons fresh lemon juice

For pastry: Mix flour and salt in large bowl. Cut in butter and shortening until mixture resembles coarse meal. Add egg and 3 tablespoons water. Stir with fork until dough begins to come together, sprinkling in additional water as necessary. Press dough together and knead lightly 2 to 3 times. Pat into disc. Wrap in plastic and refrigerate at least 30 minutes. *(Can be prepared ahead and refrigerated several days or frozen.)*

Reserve ⅓ of pastry dough; roll remaining dough out on lightly floured surface into 16-inch circle. Carefully transfer to 10½-inch quiche pan. Fit dough into pan; trim excess around edges. Crimp decoratively if desired. Roll reserved dough out into about 6 × 11-inch rectangle. Cut dough into twelve ½ × 11-inch strips. Transfer to baking sheet. Prick bottom of pastry shell several times with fork. Chill all pastry at least 30 minutes.

For filling: Bring large amount of salted water to rapid boil. Add cabbage and blanch 1 minute. Drain immediately and rinse under cold water. Drain again; pat dry. Set aside.

Melt butter in large saucepan over medium-high heat. Add onion and sauté until beginning to soften, about 3 minutes. Remove from heat. Stir in flour. Mix in lemon juice. Return to medium heat and stir for 2 minutes. Cool to room temperature.

Mix cream, ham, eggs, walnuts, parsley, lemon peel and salt and pepper in large bowl. Stir cabbage into cooled onion mixture. Add cream mixture and blend well. Taste and adjust seasoning.

Preheat oven to 425°F. Pour filling into pastry shell, spreading evenly. Carefully weave pastry strips over filled tart. Brush ends of lattice with yolk mixture. Tuck ends of lattice into tart, pressing to side of pastry shell to seal. Carefully brush top of lattice with yolk mixture. Set tart on baking sheet. Bake until filling is set and crust is golden, 30 minutes. Serve hot.

Ham Steaks in Pastry Cages

2 servings

Pastry
1 cup all purpose flour
¼ teaspoon salt
¼ cup (½ stick) butter, cut into pieces
1 tablespoon vegetable shortening
2 to 3 tablespoons ice water

Filling
¼ cup dry breadcrumbs
2 tablespoons (¼ stick) butter, melted
2 tablespoons minced fresh parsley
1 green onion, minced
1 teaspoon fresh lemon juice

½ teaspoon grated lemon peel
½ teaspoon celery seed
½ teaspoon curry powder
¼ teaspoon ground ginger
Pinch of ground red pepper
Salt and freshly ground pepper

2 5- to 6-ounce slices cooked ham, ⅜ to ½ inch thick, halved crosswise

1 egg yolk beaten with 1 tablespoon water
Sweet and Hot Mustard Sauce (see following recipe)

For pastry: Combine flour and salt in large bowl. Cut in butter and shortening until mixture resembles coarse meal. Add ice water a little at a time just until mixture holds together. Form into ball, wrap in plastic and chill 2 hours. (Can be made in processor.)

For filling: Combine all ingredients for filling in small bowl. Divide mixture between 2 half ham slices and cover with remaining slices, pressing gently.

Preheat oven to 400°F. Roll pastry out on floured surface to thickness of ⅛ inch. Cut out 2 rectangular pieces slightly larger than stuffed ham slices. Brush with egg yolk mixture. Center stuffed ham on each. Gather remaining pastry scraps into ball and reroll. Cut into ¼-inch-wide strips. Lay strips over top of ham, weaving in lattice pattern and crimping firmly into pastry base to seal. Trim any excess pastry and brush "cages" with egg yolk mixture. Bake until pastry is golden brown, about 20 to 25 minutes. Serve immediately with mustard sauce.

Sweet and Hot Mustard Sauce

Makes about ⅓ cup

3 to 4 tablespoons firmly packed brown sugar
2 to 3 tablespoons tarragon vinegar, at boiling point

1 tablespoon Dijon mustard
1 tablespoon olive oil
Salt

Combine all ingredients in small saucepan. Place over medium-low heat and cook, whisking constantly, until smooth and slightly thickened, about 2 to 3 minutes. Serve warm.

Sausage Baked in Pastry with Two Sauces
(Saucisson en Croûte aux Deux Sauces)

6 servings

1 pound boneless lean pork butt
⅓ pound fresh pork fatback *or* leaf lard
2 teaspoons salt
¼ teaspoon freshly ground pepper
1 small truffle, chopped, *or* 1 large dried shiitake mushroom, rehydrated, chopped
½ cup large pistachios, roasted and shelled

¼ cup brandy
¼ cup Madeira

1 pound puff pastry (pâte feuilletée)

1 egg yolk beaten with 1 teaspoon water

Madeira Sauce (see following recipes)
Beurre Blanc Sauce (see following recipes)

Combine pork and pork fatback in processor and grind coarsely, or use meat grinder. Transfer to bowl. Add salt and pepper and blend thoroughly. Mix in truffle. Add nuts, brandy and Madeira and blend thoroughly. Cover and chill for several hours.

Divide puff pastry into 2 portions, with one just slightly larger than the other. On lightly floured surface, roll smaller portion into rectangle ¼ inch thick. Roll meat mixture into 12-inch cylinder 2 inches thick and place lengthwise on center of rectangle. Roll remaining pastry ¼ inch thick. Lay over meat. Cut away excess pastry, leaving just enough to enclose meat (reserve scraps). Pinch seams together. Using sharp knife, make slashes around sides of pastry.

Preheat oven to 450°F. Form excess pastry scraps into ball and roll out on lightly floured surface to thickness of ¼ inch. Cut small crescents from dough. Paint pastry cylinder with egg mixture. Arrange crescents over top for decoration and paint again with egg mixture. Bake until pastry is golden brown and puffed along seam, about 25 to 35 minutes (check for doneness by inserting metal skewer into center of sausage for 1 minute and then placing it against lower lip; skewer should be hot or very warm). Let stand 5 to 10 minutes before slicing. To serve, cut into slices about 1 inch thick. Arrange 2 slices on each heated serving plate. Pour about 1 tablespoon of Madeira Sauce on 1 slice and about 1 tablespoon of Beurre Blanc Sauce on the other.

Madeira Sauce

Makes about 1 cup

6 tablespoons vegetable oil
8 to 10 pounds meaty beef and veal bones, cut into 3- to 4-inch pieces

4 cups diced onion
2 cups diced carrot
2 cups diced celery
12 whole black peppercorns
4 sprigs fresh thyme *or* 1 teaspoon dried
3 unpeeled garlic cloves, crushed
2 leeks (including 1 inch green part), thinly sliced

2 bay leaves

8 quarts water
3 to 4 cups chopped tomato
1 cup parsley leaves

¼ cup Madeira
1 tablespoon chopped truffle (optional)
2 to 2½ tablespoons unsalted butter, cut into pieces

Preheat oven to 425°F. Film bottom of large shallow roasting pan with 6 table-spoons oil. Add bones, turning to coat with oil. Roast about 2 hours, stirring and turning bones every 30 minutes.

Add next 8 ingredients and continue roasting another 30 minutes.

Transfer bones and vegetables to 12- to 16-quart stockpot. Stir 2 cups water into roasting pan, scraping up any browned bits that cling to bottom. Add to stockpot along with remaining water. Add tomato and parsley and bring to boil. Reduce heat and simmer very slowly 12 to 16 hours, skimming off any foam that accumulates on surface during first 2 to 3 hours of cooking.

Strain stock, reserving 2 cups and refrigerating or freezing remainder for later use. Pour 2 cups stock into small saucepan and boil over high heat until reduced to 1½ cups. Add Madeira and continue boiling until sauce is reduced to 1 cup. Turn heat to low and add truffle. Whisk in butter 1 piece at a time, beating well after each addition. Serve immediately.

Beurre Blanc Sauce

Makes about 1½ cups

½ cup dry white wine (preferably Chablis)	½ cup whipping cream
2 tablespoons minced shallot	1 tablespoon Dijon mustard
16 tablespoons (2 sticks) unsalted butter, well chilled	¼ teaspoon salt
	⅛ teaspoon freshly ground pepper

Combine wine and shallot in small saucepan. Cook over medium heat until wine is reduced to about 2 tablespoons. Remove from heat and whisk in butter 1 tablespoon at a time, incorporating completely before adding another tablespoon. After adding 2 or 3 tablespoons, return pan to very low heat and whisk in remaining butter in same manner (sauce will be consistency of light mayonnaise). Beat in cream, mustard, salt and pepper and blend well.

❦ Braising and Poaching

Prince's Pot (Prinzentopf)

5 to 6 servings

4 large tomatoes, peeled, cored, seeded and chopped	1 pound fresh asparagus, trimmed, *or* 1 10-ounce package frozen spears, cut into 2½-inch pieces
1½ pounds boneless pork loin, trimmed of all fat, cut into ½-inch slices and patted dry	
Salt and freshly ground pepper	*Sauce*
2 tablespoons (¼ stick) butter	1½ tablespoons butter
2 tablespoons vegetable oil	1½ tablespoons all purpose flour
1 cup minced cooked smoked ham	½ cup whipping cream
1 small onion, finely chopped	1 tablespoon catsup
3 medium leeks (white part only), quartered lengthwise and cut into 2½-inch lengths	Salt

Spread half of chopped tomatoes in bottom of 3- to 4-quart Dutch oven or flame-proof casserole. Sprinkle pork with salt and pepper. Melt 1 tablespoon butter with 1 tablespoon oil in heavy large skillet over medium heat. Add pork and brown well on all sides. Drain well; arrange over tomatoes. Melt 1 tablespoon butter with 1 tablespoon oil in same skillet over medium heat. Add ham and onion and cook 3 to 4 minutes. Sprinkle over pork (do not wipe out skillet). Top with remaining chopped tomatoes. Cover, place over low heat and simmer 45 minutes, adding 1 or 2 tablespoons water if necessary to prevent sticking. Arrange leeks over pork. Top with layer of asparagus. Cover and cook until vegetables are crisp-tender, 15 minutes.

For sauce: About 5 minutes before vegetables are done, melt 1½ tablespoons butter in same skillet. Stir in flour and mix until smooth. Cook 1 minute. Gradually drain liquid from Dutch oven into flour mixture, stirring until sauce is smooth. Gradually add cream, catsup and salt. Drain stew again and transfer to tureen, or serve from Dutch oven. (Juices from vegetables will settle in bottom of Dutch oven if allowed to stand. Drain before adding sauce or stew will be watery.) Pour sauce over and serve.

White Bean One-pot (Weisse Bohnen Eintopf)

H6 to 8 servings

2 cups quick-cooking dried Great Northern beans, rinsed and drained
5 to 6 cups water

3 tablespoons butter
2 tablespoons vegetable oil
1 large onion, chopped
1 garlic clove, minced
½ cup coarsely chopped fresh parsley
3 carrots, diced
1 large tomato, peeled, cored, seeded and coarsely chopped
1¼ cups finely diced smoked ham (preferably country ham)

¼ cup diced celery root *or* chopped celery (with leaves)
1 small bay leaf, bruised
¾ teaspoon salt
¼ teaspoon freshly ground pepper
¼ teaspoon Hungarian sweet paprika
⅛ teaspoon dried thyme
⅛ teaspoon dried marjoram
Generous pinch of ground cloves

1 pound German rindwurst *or* bockwurst (*or* smoked knockwurst *or* frankfurters), cut into ⅜-inch slices
Freshly ground pepper

Combine beans and 5 cups water in large Dutch oven or stockpot and bring to boil over medium heat. Cover and let cook for 1 hour.

Melt 2 tablespoons butter with 1 tablespoon oil in heavy large skillet over medium heat. Add onion, garlic and parsley and cook 6 to 7 minutes. Transfer 2 cups of beans to processor and puree until smooth. Return to Dutch oven. Add onion mixture and next 11 ingredients. Reduce heat to low, cover and simmer until vegetables are tender, about 1 hour, adding remaining 1 cup water as necessary to preventing sticking.

About 5 minutes before vegetables are done, melt remaining 1 tablespoon butter with 1 tablespoon oil in same skillet over medium heat. Add sausage slices and brown on all sides. Drain well. Taste soup and adjust seasoning. Transfer to tureen or serve from Dutch oven. Garnish top with sausage slices and pepper.

Butcher's One-pot with Sauerkraut
(Schlächttopf mit Sauerkraut)

5 servings

3 thick slices bacon (preferably country cured), cut in half	1 large bay leaf, bruised
½ pound small country sausages	¾ teaspoon caraway seed
	¼ teaspoon freshly ground pepper
1 large onion, chopped	4 medium potatoes, peeled and cut into ¼-inch slices
1 medium carrot, finely diced	Salt and freshly ground pepper
1 tablespoon minced fresh parsley	
2 pounds canned sauerkraut, rinsed and drained	1 pound assorted German sausages (blockwurst, wienerwurst, blutwurst and knockwurst)
10 juniper berries, crushed	1 tablespoon snipped fresh chives
⅔ cup water	
½ cup dry German white wine	

Cook bacon in large Dutch oven or flameproof casserole over medium-high heat until crisp. Remove with slotted spoon and drain on paper towels. Add country sausages to same pan and brown thoroughly on all sides. Remove with slotted spoon and drain.

Combine onion, carrot and parsley in same pan and cook over medium heat 4 to 5 minutes. Add sauerkraut, juniper berries, water, wine, bay leaf, caraway seed and ¼ teaspoon pepper and mix well. Reduce heat to low. Arrange potatoes over sauerkraut and season lightly with salt and pepper. Top potatoes with bacon slices and country sausages. Cover and cook gently over low heat about 20 minutes, watching carefully to prevent sticking.

Just before serving, arrange assorted sausages over top of casserole. Cover and cook until sausages are lightly steamed *(do not allow to split)*, about 10 minutes. Transfer to soup tureen or serve from Dutch oven. Sprinkle with chives and serve immediately.

Herb-glazed Pork Chops

2 servings

2 1-inch-thick pork chops	½ cup chopped onion
Coarse salt	¼ cup diced carrot
Cracked black pepper	½ cup beef stock
½ teaspoon dried thyme	¼ cup dry white wine
½ teaspoon paprika	
¼ teaspoon dried marjoram	⅓ cup whipping cream
	¼ cup diced pimiento
1 tablespoon butter	½ teaspoon crushed green peppercorns, rinsed and drained
1 tablespoon olive oil	Salt and freshly ground pepper
1 large garlic clove	

Sprinkle pork chops on both sides with coarse salt and cracked black pepper. Mix thyme, paprika and marjoram in small bowl. Press herb mixture onto both sides of pork chops.

Melt butter with oil in heavy small skillet over medium-low heat. Add garlic and stir until golden; discard. Add pork and brown on both sides. Remove from skillet and set aside. Add onion and carrot and stir until lightly browned, 2 to 3 minutes. Blend in stock and wine and bring to boil. Return pork to skillet. Cover and simmer gently until thermometer inserted in thickest portion of chops registers 170°F, about 25 minutes.

Remove pork chops from skillet. Increase heat to high. Whisk in cream, scraping up any browned bits, and boil until sauce thickens, about 2 minutes. Stir in pimiento and peppercorns. Season with salt and pepper. Spoon sauce over chops and serve immediately.

Provençal Pork in Fennel Cups

Here are the special flavors of southern France in an easy-to-do main dish. Start with a salad and serve the pork with hot buttered noodles or potatoes. And don't forget bread for dunking in the sauce. Accompany with a dry and fruity Johannisberg Ries-ling. For a variation, add 1 pound of cooked mild Ital-ian sausage to the pork during the last 10 minutes of cooking time.

4 servings

2 to 3 tablespoons olive oil
2 pounds lean pork from sirloin, leg *or* shoulder, trimmed of fat and cut into 1½-inch cubes
1 medium onion, chopped
1 to 1½ tablespoons freshly grated orange peel
1 large garlic clove, minced
¼ teaspoon *each* chopped fresh thyme, sage, rosemary, basil and savory *or* ¼ teaspoon *each* dried
1 tablespoon all purpose flour

½ cup dry vermouth
4 anchovy fillets
2 cups beef stock

¼ cup mild-cured Greek *or* Italian black olives, pitted
1 tablespoon capers, rinsed and drained
Salt and freshly ground pepper

1 to 1½ pounds large fresh fennel bulbs*
2½ ounces Gruyère cheese

Heat 2 tablespoons olive oil in heavy nonaluminum skillet over medium-high heat. Add pork in batches *(do not crowd)* and brown on all sides, adding more oil if necessary. Transfer pork to 3- to 4-quart saucepan. Pour off all but thin layer of oil from skillet. Add onion, place over medium heat and cook until softened and just beginning to color, about 3 minutes, stirring frequently. Add orange peel, garlic and herbs and stir about 30 seconds. Sprinkle with flour and stir 30 more seconds, watching carefully so flour does not brown. Blend in vermouth and anchovies, scraping up any browned bits, and bring to boil. Let boil until mixture is reduced by about half. Blend in stock and return to boil. Pour mixture over pork. Place over medium-high heat and bring to gentle simmer. Reduce heat to low, cover and cook until pork is tender, about 1½ hours.

Stir olives and capers into stew. Season to taste with salt and pepper. Cool; cover and refrigerate 1 to 3 days. (Bring to room temperature before continuing.)

Trim off tops of fennel bulbs, reserving about 2 tablespoons of feathery leaves. Using small sharp knife, remove core at base of bulb. Trim base and separate stalks. Add enough water to steamer or large pot fitted with steamer rack to come just below rack. Place over high heat and bring to boil. Add fennel stalks and steam until crisp-tender, about 10 minutes. Let cool. Refrigerate fennel for up to 2 days.

Preheat oven to 350°F. Butter shallow 8 × 12-inch baking dish. Arrange fennel stalks in dish, rounded side down, overlapping if necessary. Sprinkle reserved fennel leaves over top. Spoon stew into fennel "cups." Bake until bubbling, about 30 minutes. Sprinkle with cheese and continue baking until cheese is melted, about 10 minutes. Serve immediately.

*Six small hollowed-out green or red bell peppers can be substituted for fennel; steam until crisp-tender before filling.

Greek Pork and Collards

This version of collards, tomatoes and pork spareribs can be prepared several hours ahead and reheated before serving.

4 servings

2 tablespoons (¼ stick) butter
2 tablespoons olive oil
2 pounds pork spareribs, cut crosswise into 1-inch pieces and patted dry
1 large onion, chopped

1 14½-ounce can tomatoes, undrained
1 teaspoon sugar
3 pounds collard greens, stemmed
Salt and freshly ground pepper

Melt butter with oil in heavy Dutch oven over medium-high heat. Add spareribs and brown on all sides. Reduce heat to low. Add onion, cover and cook until translucent, stirring frequently, about 10 minutes. Mix in tomatoes and sugar and bring to boil. Arrange collard greens atop ribs. Season with salt and pepper. Cover and simmer 10 minutes. Stir greens into liquid. Cover and simmer until collards and ribs are tender, about 45 minutes. Adjust seasoning. Serve immediately.

Pork Steaks with Cardamom and Fresh Grapes

A robust country dish that is best mellowed overnight before serving.

8 servings

3 tablespoons vegetable oil, or more
8 pounds well-marbled pork steaks *or* cutlets from sirloin *or* leg, cut to thickness of about 1 inch (3½ pounds total)

4 medium onions, thinly sliced
2 large garlic cloves, minced
Seeds of 16 cardamom pods, ground (1½ teaspoons ground)

¼ teaspoon ground coriander
¼ cup brandy
1 tablespoon cider vinegar *or* wine vinegar
1 cup dry red wine
1 cup meat *or* poultry stock

Salt and freshly ground pepper
½ cup red grapes, halved and seeded
1 tablespoon minced chives *or* green onion (garnish)

Heat 3 tablespoons oil in heavy nonaluminum large skillet over medium-high heat. Add pork in batches *(do not crowd)* and brown, adding oil as necessary. Remove pork from skillet.

Pour off all but about 2 tablespoons fat from skillet. Reduce heat to low, add onions, cover and cook until softened, about 10 minutes, stirring occasionally. Increase heat to medium and stir until browned, 5 to 7 minutes. Stir in garlic, cardamom and coriander and cook 2 minutes; *do not brown.* Pour in brandy and vinegar and boil, scraping up any browned bits, until reduced to glaze. Add wine and boil 4 minutes. Blend in stock and bring to simmer. Add pork and spoon liquid over. Cover and simmer gently until pork is tender, about 45 minutes. *(If preparing ahead and reheating, slightly undercook pork at this point.)*

Skim fat from surface. *(Can be prepared 1 day ahead to this point, cooled and refrigerated. Reheat pork gently in simmering liquid before continuing.)* Transfer pork to serving platter. Simmer liquid until thickened to saucelike consistency. Season with salt and pepper. Stir in grapes and heat through. Pour sauce over pork. Top with chives and serve.

Pork with Pears

Present this dish on a bed of rice.

6 to 8 servings

1 to 3 tablespoons safflower oil
1½ pounds lean pork, trimmed, well dried and cut into 1-inch cubes
2 cups water
½ cup cider vinegar
2 tablespoons soy sauce
1 garlic clove, minced
   Salt and freshly ground pepper

⅓ cup sugar
⅓ cup fresh lemon juice
2 tablespoons plus 1 teaspoon cornstarch

4 green onions, cut into ½-inch pieces
½ green bell pepper, cut into 1-inch strips
1 celery stalk, cut diagonally into 1-inch pieces
1 5-ounce can water chestnuts, drained and halved
3 firm ripe pears, peeled, cored and sliced

Heat 1 tablespoon oil in heavy large skillet over medium-high heat. Cook pork in batches (*do not crowd*) and sauté until browned, adding more oil as necessary. Return all pork to skillet. Add water, vinegar, soy sauce and garlic. Season with salt and pepper. Cover and simmer until meat is tender, 30 to 40 minutes.

Blend sugar, lemon juice and cornstarch in small bowl. Stir into pork mixture. Cook, stirring constantly, until sauce is clear and thickened. Add green onion, green pepper, celery and water chestnuts. Cover and simmer 1 minute. Fold in pears. Serve hot.

Braised Country-style Ribs with Wine, Kraut and Calvados

These ribs can be prepared up to 2 days ahead and reheated slowly over low heat.

4 to 6 servings

4 cups water
⅔ cup salt
5 tablespoons firmly packed brown sugar
3 whole cloves
1 bay leaf
1 heaping teaspoon saltpeter (optional)
½ heaping teaspoon juniper berries
½ heaping teaspoon whole allspice
½ heaping teaspoon white peppercorns
½ heaping teaspoon dried thyme
¼ teaspoon whole yellow mustard seed

3 pounds country-style pork spareribs
4 cups dry white wine

3 tablespoons vegetable oil
1 large onion, chopped
1½ pounds sauerkraut, well rinsed and drained
¼ cup Calvados *or* applejack
1 cup dry white wine (preferably Alsatian Sylvaner)
½ cup unsalted beef stock
3 juniper berries, lightly crushed
   Freshly ground pepper

Combine first 11 ingredients in 4-quart nonaluminum saucepan and bring to boil over medium heat. Increase heat to high, cover partially and let boil 3 minutes. Remove from heat and skim off any foam that has accumulated on surface. Let cool completely to room temperature.

Strain brine through cheesecloth into 5-quart pottery or stainless steel crock. Add ribs and 4 cups wine. Weight with plate to keep meat submerged in brine. Let stand in cool place 2 days to cure.

Heat oil in heavy 5-quart saucepan over medium-high heat. Add ribs in batches (*do not crowd*) and brown well on all sides; set aside. Add onion to saucepan and brown lightly. Stir in sauerkraut and Calvados and cook 2 minutes, stirring constantly. Add 1 cup wine, stock and 3 juniper berries and blend well. Reduce heat so mixture simmers. Bury ribs in mixture; cover and simmer until meat is tender, skimming fat as necessary, about 1 to 1½ hours. (If mixture seems too thin, remove ribs and reduce liquid over high heat until sauerkraut is just barely moist.) Season to taste with pepper. Arrange sauerkraut on platter and top with ribs.

Ragout of Pork with Rosemary

Sautéed new potatoes or buttered noodles are appropriate accompaniments.

5 to 6 servings

3 pounds lean pork butt, cut into 1½-inch cubes
Salt and freshly ground pepper
2 to 3 tablespoons vegetable oil
1 tablespoon butter

2 cups minced onion
1 teaspoon minced garlic
1 28-ounce can Italian plum tomatoes, thoroughly drained and chopped, *or* 4 large ripe tomatoes, peeled, seeded and finely chopped
1 tablespoon tomato paste
1 cup dry white wine
1½ to 2 cups brown chicken stock

Bouquet garni (1 large sprig fresh thyme, 1 large sprig fresh rosemary, 1 large sprig parsley and 1 bay leaf, tied together in a cheesecloth bag)

2 cups peeled cubed fresh turnip
1 cup fresh peas (about 1 pound unshelled)
1 tablespoon potato flour *or* arrowroot mixed with a little stock
1 large garlic clove, crushed
Fresh rosemary
Minced fresh parsley (garnish)

Pat meat dry with paper towels. Sprinkle with salt and pepper. Heat 2 tablespoons oil with butter in heavy large skillet over medium-high heat. Add pork in small batches *(do not crowd)* and brown on all sides. Transfer to heatproof casserole dish.

Position rack in center of oven and preheat to 350°F. If fat in skillet has burned, discard and add another tablespoon of oil to skillet. Place over medium heat. Add onion and garlic and sauté until softened and lightly browned, scraping up any bits clinging to bottom of pan. Add tomatoes and tomato paste and bring to boil. Cook until most of liquid has evaporated, about 3 to 4 minutes. Blend in wine. Return to boil and cook until wine is reduced by half. Add to pork. Add stock and bouquet garni. Cover and braise until meat is just tender but not falling apart, about 1½ hours. Season to taste with salt and pepper.

Discard bouquet garni. Remove meat. Strain pan juices through fine sieve. Return juices to casserole and bring just to boil over direct heat. Add meat, turnip and peas, cover and simmer until vegetables are done. Whisk in potato flour and continue mixing until sauce heavily coats spoon. Taste and adjust seasoning. Stir in remaining garlic and additional rosemary to taste. Transfer to serving bowl and sprinkle with parsley.

Braised Pork in the Mode of Caen

A variation of a classic Norman dish. Serve with dry French cider or a fruity white Riesling. Save the cooked pig's feet, which are used to give body and character to the sauce; they are delicious rolled in flour, beaten egg and dry bread-crumbs and grilled.

8 to 10 servings

2 pig's feet
3 ounces thick-cut smoked bacon, coarsely chopped

3 tablespoons clarified butter
4½ to 5 pounds boneless pork from Boston butt *or* fresh ham, cut into 1-inch cubes

2 pounds carrot, halved lengthwise and cut into 2-inch lengths
8 medium onions, cut into ⅓-inch rings
1 cup Calvados *or* applejack
3 cups hard cider

3 cups dry white wine
3 cups meat *or* poultry stock
2 large garlic cloves, minced
2 bay leaves, broken
4 3-inch sprigs fresh thyme *or* ¼ teaspoon dried
2 heaping teaspoons fresh tarragon *or* ⅔ teaspoon dried
⅛ teaspoon salt, or to taste
⅛ teaspoon freshly ground pepper
   Pinch of ground red pepper
   Pinch of ground cloves

   Boiled potatoes

Bring pig's feet and 16 cups water to boil in large saucepan. Reduce heat and simmer 30 minutes. Drain and rinse. Blanch bacon in boiling water 5 minutes. Drain and pat dry.

Cook bacon with butter in heavy large skillet over medium heat until crisp. Transfer to paper towels using slotted spoon. Add pork to skillet in batches *(do not crowd)* and brown on all sides. Transfer to 6- to 7-quart casserole.

Pour off all but 3 tablespoons fat in skillet. Increase heat to medium high. Add carrot and sauté until beginning to brown, about 5 minutes. Mix in onions and cook until golden, about 6 minutes, stirring frequently. Add Calvados and boil until reduced to glaze, scraping up any browned bits. Pour in cider and wine and boil until reduced by half. Spoon over pork. Add pig's feet, bacon and remaining ingredients except potatoes to casserole and bring to simmer. Cover tightly and cook until pork is tender, about 2 hours. Degrease liquid. *(Can be prepared 3 days ahead to this point. Cover and refrigerate. Reheat over medium heat.)*

Transfer meat and vegetables to heated serving bowl using slotted spoon (reserve pig's feet for another use). Discard bay leaves. Tent with foil. Boil liquid until reduced to saucelike consistency. Pour over pork and vegetables. Serve immediately with boiled potatoes.

Red-cooked Pork Hock

Use small front pork hocks, which are particularly tender, if they are available.

2 main-course servings or 4 servings as part of a multi-course Chinese meal

3 pounds pork (ham) hock (2 to 3 small *or* 1 large)
1½ cups water
½ cup rock sugar *or* firmly packed brown sugar
¼ cup dark soy sauce

1 pound miniature bok choy (ching gong choi),* yellow leaves discarded, *or* broccoli florets
¼ cup vegetable oil
2 teaspoons salt

Place pork in heavy medium saucepan. Add water, sugar and soy sauce and bring to boil. Reduce heat to medium, cover and cook at low boil until pork is tender when pierced with chopsticks and meat is almost falling off bone, turning every

30 minutes, about 2 hours for small hocks or 3 hours for 1 large. *(Can be prepared 1 day ahead to this point. Cool mixture to room temperature, then cover and refrigerate.)*

Meanwhile, rinse bok choy under cold water, carefully pulling stems open to rinse inside. Boil bok choy in large pot of water with oil and salt until crisp-tender, about 3 minutes. Drain.

Degrease pork cooking liquid. Cook pork and liquid over high heat until liquid is reduced to syrup, basting constantly, about 5 minutes. Arrange pork in center of platter. Surround with bok choy. Pour sauce over pork and serve immediately.

* Available in oriental markets.

Stuffed Pork Chops from Bern

A robust do-ahead dish that is delicious with braised Belgian endive or sautéed green beans. Offer a Beaujolais or Gewürztraminer alongside.

4 servings

2 tablespoons (¼ stick) butter
5 ounces mushrooms, sliced
2 large shallots, minced
3 tablespoons dry red wine
Salt and freshly ground pepper
2 ounces Gruyère cheese, grated

4 1¼- to 1½-inch-thick blade end pork loin chops

4 tablespoons clarified butter
1 cup minced onion
½ cup minced carrot
½ cup minced celery
1 cup dry white wine (preferably Riesling)

1 tablespoon tomato paste
8 bay leaves, broken
1 large garlic clove, minced
⅛ teaspoon dried thyme
2 cups unsalted meat *or* poultry stock

½ cup whipping cream
4 tablespoons snipped fresh chives
2 teaspoons fresh lemon juice, or more
Salt and freshly ground pepper

Melt 2 tablespoons butter in heavy medium skillet over medium-high heat. Add mushrooms and sauté until light brown. Add shallots and sauté 30 seconds. Pour in red wine and boil until reduced to glaze. Season with salt and pepper. Cool to room temperature. Blend in Gruyère. *(Can be prepared 1 day ahead. Cover and refrigerate.)*

Make 1½-inch-long slit in center of edge of each chop opposite rib bone. With knife inserted in slit, cut arc, creating wide pocket inside chop with small opening. Stuff mushroom mixture into pockets. Press to close.

Preheat oven to 325°F. Heat clarified butter in heavy large skillet over medium-high heat. Pat chops dry and brown on both sides. Transfer to shallow baking dish. Pour off all but 3 tablespoons fat from skillet. Sauté onion, carrot and celery in same skillet over medium heat until golden, about 5 minutes. Add white wine, tomato paste, bay leaves, garlic and thyme. Boil until liquid is reduced to glaze, scraping up any browned bits, about 12 minutes. Pour in stock and boil until reduced by half. Spoon over chops. Cover lightly with foil. Bake until chops are tender, about 1¼ hours.

Strain sauce into skillet, pressing on solids to extract as much juice as possible; degrease. Tent chops with foil. Boil sauce until reduced by ⅓. Add cream and boil until sauce thickens enough to coat spoon. Add 3 tablespoons chives, lemon juice to taste and salt and pepper. Divide chops among heated plates. Spoon some sauce atop chops. Sprinkle with chives. Serve immediately. Serve remaining sauce separately.

Champagne Sausage with Sauce Piquante

Leftover Champagne? This is the dish. Form into patties or use casings.

4 servings (about ten 5-inch sausages)

¾ pound trimmed pork shoulder *or* loin, cut into ½ × 1¾-inch strips
¾ pound trimmed beef chuck *or* round, cut into ½ × 1¾-inch strips
½ pound trimmed pork fat, cut into ½ × 1¾-inch strips
2 medium garlic cloves
1 large shallot
1½ teaspoons minced fresh marjoram *or* ½ teaspoon dried
½ teaspoon paprika
⅛ teaspoon ground cloves
2 teaspoons salt

¼ teaspoon coarsely ground pepper
¼ cup walnuts, coarsely chopped (optional)
⅓ cup (5⅓ tablespoons) brut Champagne *or* dry red wine

1 tablespoon butter (for patties)
1 tablespoon vegetable oil (for patties)

Sauce Piquante (see following recipe)
Sprigs fresh tarragon (garnish)

If using casings, rinse and soak in tepid water for 1 hour. Freeze pork, beef and fat for 30 minutes, then grind through fine blade of meat grinder with garlic and shallot. Mix in marjoram, paprika, cloves, salt, pepper and walnuts. Stir in Champagne 1 tablespoon at a time. Cover and refrigerate for 1 hour.

Form sausage mixture into patties or stuff into casings and tie or twist into 10 links. Hang in cool spot until dry or refrigerate on rack, turning occasionally, for 12 to 24 hours.

To cook links, bring 10 cups water to simmer in Dutch oven or large saucepan. Add sausages, cover and poach gently until cooked through, 20 minutes. Remove sausages; prick with fork.

To cook patties, melt butter with oil in heavy large skillet over medium-high heat. Add sausages in batches and fry on both sides until browned and cooked through. Drain on paper towels.

To serve, spoon Sauce Piquante in center of 4 heated plates. Arrange sausage on top and garnish with tarragon sprigs.

Sauce Piquante

This sauce can be made a day ahead.

Makes about 1⅓ cups

2 cups beef stock
½ cup brut Champagne *or* Madeira
¼ cup tarragon vinegar
1 large shallot, minced
2 tablespoons Cognac
2 tablespoons minced cornichons
2 tablespoons minced capers, rinsed and drained

Salt and freshly ground pepper
1½ tablespoons minced fresh parsley
1½ tablespoons minced fresh tarragon *or* 1¼ teaspoons dried
1½ tablespoons minced fresh chervil (optional)
2 tablespoons (¼ stick) butter

Boil stock, Champagne, vinegar and shallot in small saucepan until liquid is reduced by half. Stir in Cognac, cornichons, capers and salt and pepper. Just before serving, place over low heat and stir in parsley, tarragon and chervil. Whisk in butter 1 tablespoon at a time, mixing until sauce is slightly thickened.

Caldo Gallego

This is a hearty, stewlike soup. Serve with a green salad and hot, crusty bread.

4 servings

8 ounces dried small white beans
¼ pound salt pork
¼ pound smoked ham, diced

6 cups water
¼ pound chorizo (Mexican sausage), thinly sliced
2 cups loosely packed shredded cabbage

½ pound turnips (including greens), peeled and chopped
1 medium onion, thinly sliced
1 large potato, peeled and cubed (optional)
Salt and freshly ground pepper

Combine beans, salt pork and ham in medium bowl with enough water to cover. Let stand overnight at room temperature. Drain well.

Bring 6 cups water to boil in large saucepan or Dutch oven over medium-high heat. Add bean mixture. Reduce heat to low, cover and simmer 1½ hours. Add chorizo and simmer another 30 minutes. Stir in remaining vegetables and continue simmering until liquid is reduced and thickened, about 30 to 60 minutes. Discard salt pork. Season to taste with salt and pepper.

Italian Sausage

4 servings (about nine 5- to 6-inch sausages)

1½ pounds trimmed pork shoulder *or* loin, cut into ½ × 1¾-inch strips
½ pound trimmed pork fat, cut into ½ × 1¾-inch strips

2¼ teaspoons fennel seed
1 to 3 dried small red chilies
1½ teaspoons minced fresh marjoram *or* ½ teaspoon dried
½ teaspoon (scant) whole black peppercorns

½ teaspoon minced garlic
¼ teaspoon paprika
2 teaspoons salt
⅓ cup (5⅓ tablespoons) dry red wine

1 tablespoon butter
1 tablespoon vegetable oil

Rinse sausage casings and soak in tepid water for 1 hour. Freeze pork and fat for 30 minutes, then grind through fine blade of grinder.

Coarsely crush fennel, chilies, marjoram and peppercorns in mortar. Stir into meat with garlic, paprika and salt. Stir in wine 1 tablespoon at a time. Cover and refrigerate 1 hour.

Stuff sausage mixture into casings. Tie or twist into 9 links. Hang in cool spot until dry or refrigerate on a rack, turning occasionally, 12 to 24 hours.

Bring 10 cups water to simmer in Dutch oven or large saucepan. Add sausages, cover and poach gently 15 minutes. Drain sausages well, discarding poaching liquid. Pat sausages dry. Heat butter and oil in same saucepan. Add sausages and sauté over medium heat until brown.

Bockwurst

This mildly seasoned sausage is well complemented by vegetable medley and cold beer.

4 servings (about 8 sausages)

¾ pound trimmed pork shoulder *or* loin, cut into ½ × 1¾-inch strips
¾ pound veal shoulder *or* breast, cut into ½ × 1¾-inch strips
½ pound trimmed pork fat, cut into ½ × 1¾-inch strips
1½ tablespoons minced chives
¾ teaspoon paprika
½ teaspoon ground ginger
¼ teaspoon ground cardamom
¼ teaspoon freshly grated nutmeg
⅛ teaspoon cinnamon
2 teaspoons salt
¼ teaspoon freshly ground pepper
3 tablespoons whipping cream, milk *or* dry white wine

2½ quarts veal stock *or* water

Mustard Wine Sauce (see following recipe)

Rinse sausage casings and soak in tepid water for 1 hour. Freeze pork, veal and fat for 30 minutes, then grind through fine blade of grinder. Mix in chives, paprika, ginger, cardamom, nutmeg, cinnamon, salt and pepper. Stir in cream 1 tablespoon at a time. Cover and refrigerate for 1 hour.

Stuff sausage mixture into casings. Tie or twist into 8 links. Hang in cool spot until dry or refrigerate on rack, turning occasionally, 12 to 24 hours.

Bring stock to simmer in Dutch oven or large saucepan. Add sausages, cover and poach gently until cooked through, about 20 minutes.

To serve, arrange sausages on heated serving platter. Serve with Mustard Wine Sauce.

Mustard Wine Sauce

This sauce can be made a day ahead.

Makes about 1½ cups

2½ cups veal *or* beef stock
½ cup red wine
¼ cup white wine vinegar
1 tablespoon coarse stone-ground mustard
Salt and freshly ground pepper
1 tablespoon minced chives
2 tablespoons (¼ stick) butter

Boil stock, wine and vinegar in small saucepan until reduced by half. Stir in mustard and season with salt and pepper. Just before serving, place over low heat and stir in chives. Whisk in butter 1 tablespoon at a time, mixing until butter is melted and sauce is smooth.

🍂 Index

Credits and Acknowledgments

The following people contributed the recipes included in this book:

Dee Andronico
Nancy Baggett
Beamreach Restaurant, Kauia, Hawaii
Natalie Berkowitz and Judith Lebson
Nic and Nancy Boghosian
Marcia and William Bond
Dale Booher and Lisa Stamm
Cameron Boyd
Naila Britain-Callahan
Patricia Brooks
Martha Buller
Anna Teresa Callen
Casa Marra, New Haven, Connecticut
Cattails, Palm Springs, California
Ginger Chang
The Coach House, New York, New York
Peter and Susan Coe
Darrell Corti
La Côte Basque, New York, New York, Jean-Jacques Rachou, chef-owner
Ruth O. Crassweller
Diane Darrow and Tom Maresca
Deirdre Davis and Linda Marino
Déjà-Vu, Philadelphia, Pennsylvania
Mary and Henri Dorra
Myra Dorros
L'Ermitage, Los Angeles, California
L'Espérance, Saint-Père-sous-Vézelay, France, Marc Meneau, chef
Joe Famularo
Fortune Garden Restaurant, New York, New York
Le Français, Wheeling, Illinois
Cora Gemil
Marion Gorman
Bob and Beverly Green
Freddi Greenberg
Greenlake Grill, Seattle, Washington
Anne Greer
Sharon Guizzetti
Jim Holmes
Jackie Horwitz
Bill Hughes
J.P.'s Porterhouse Too, Latham, New York
Linda Johnson
Ruth Hartley Johnson

Jane Helsel Joseph
Julie's Ristorante, Ogunquit, Maine
Madeleine Kamman
Kan's, San Francisco, California
Barbara Karoff
Lynne Kasper
Kristina Korabiak
Leo, Santa Croce, Italy
Lodge Alley Inn, New Orleans, Louisiana
John Loring
Saleh Makar
Theonie Mark
Copeland Marks
Perla Meyers
Jinx and Jefferson Morgan
The Old Greenfield Inn, Lancaster, Pennsylvania
Old Plank Road Depot, High Point, North Carolina
L'Orangerie, Los Angeles, California
Philipps on the Lake, Minocqua, Wisconsin
Dale and Susie Pierson
Ponte's, New York, New York
Queen Mary, Long Beach, California
The Roof, Salt Lake City, Utah
Salishan's Gourmet Room, Salishan Lodge, Gleneden Beach, Oregon, Bill Jung, executive chef
The San Francisco, Sydney, Australia
Richard Sax
Joan Shaw
Edena Sheldon
Patricia Skinner
Shirley Slater
Bonnie Stern
Anne Sullivan
The Summit at Harrah's, Lake Tahoe, California
The Village Smithy, Glencoe, Illinois
Vintage 1847, Hermann, Missouri
Elaine Wally
Jan Weimer
Westin Hotel, Boston, Massachusetts
Lynn Wolkerstorfer
Gloria Zimmerman

Additional text was supplied by:

Rita Leinwand, *Bearnaise, Braising, Brown Stock*
Jan Weimer, *Classic Brown Sauce and Variations*

Food styled for photographs by:

Jean E. Carey, cover, Pot-au-feu, Veal Chops en Papillote with Leeks, Carrots, Parsnips and Spiced Butter

Props styled for photographs by:

Karen Blockland, cover, Pot-au-feu, Veal Chops en Papillote with Leeks, Carrots, Parsnips and Spiced Butter

Special thanks to:

Marilou Vaughan, *Editor, Bon Appétit*
Bernard Rotondo, *Art Director, Bon Appétit*
William J. Garry, *Managing Editor, Bon Appétit*
Barbara Varnum, *Articles Editor, Bon Appétit*
Jane Matyas, *Associate Food Editor, Bon Appétit*
Brenda Koplin, *Copy Editor, Bon Appétit*
Judith Strausberg, *Copy Editor, Bon Appétit*
Robin G. Richardson, *Research Coordinator, Bon Appétit*
Leslie A. Dame, *Assistant Editor, Bon Appétit*
Donna Clipperton, *Manager, Rights and Permissions, Knapp Communications Corporation*
Karen Legier, *Rights and Permissions Coordinator, Knapp Communications Corporation*
Rose Grant
David Groves
Tyra Mead
Mary Nadler
Sylvia Tidwell

The Knapp Press
is a wholly owned subsidiary of
KNAPP COMMUNICATIONS CORPORATION.
Chairman and Chief Executive Officer:
   Cleon T. Knapp
President: H. Stephen Cranston
Senior Vice-Presidents:
   Rosalie Bruno *(New Venture
      Development)*
   Betsy Wood Knapp *(MIS Electronic
      Media)*
   Harry Myers *(Magazine Group
      Publisher)*
   William J. N. Porter *(Corporate
      Product Sales)*
   Paige Rense *(Editorial)*
   L. James Wade, Jr. *(Finance)*

THE KNAPP PRESS

President: Alice Bandy; *Administrative Assistant:*
Beth Bell; *Editor:* Norman Kolpas; *Managing
Editor:* Pamela Mosher; *Associate Editors:* Colleen
Dunn Bates, Jan Koot, Diane Rossen Worthington;
Assistant Editor: Nancy D. Roberts; *Editorial
Assistant:* Teresa Roupe; *Art Director:* Paula
Schlosser; *Designer:* Robin Murawski; *Marketing
Designer:* Barbara Kosoff; *Book Production
Manager:* Larry Cooke; *Book Production
Coordinators:* Veronica Losorelli, Joan Valentine;
Financial Manager: Joseph Goodman; *Assistant
Finance Manager:* Kerri Culbertson; *Financial
Assistant:* Julie Mason; *Fulfillment Services
Manager:* Virginia Parry; *Director of Public
Relations:* Jan B. Fox; *Marketing Assistants:*
Dolores Briqueleur, Randy Levin; *Promotions
Managers:* Joanne Denison, Nina Gerwin; *Special
Sales Manager:* Lynn Blocker; *Special Sales
Coordinator:* Amy Hershman

This book is set in Sabon, a face designed by Jan Teischold in 1967 and based on early
fonts engraved by Garamond and Granjon.

Composition was on the Mergenthaler Linotron 202 by Graphic Typesetting Service.

Series design by Paula Schlosser.

Text stock: Knapp Cookbook Opaque, basis 65. Color plate stock: Mead Northcote
basis 70. Both furnished by WWF Paper Corporation West.

Color separations by NEC Incorporated.

Printing and binding by R. R. Donnelley and Sons.